Leadership in the Way of the Cross

Leadership in the Way of the Cross

Forging Ministry from the Crucible of Crisis

SHERWOOD G. LINGENFELTER

CASCADE *Books* · Eugene, Oregon

LEADERSHIP IN THE WAY OF THE CROSS
Forging Ministry from the Crucible of Crisis

Cascade Books
An Imprint of Wipf and Stock Publishers
199 W. 8th Ave., Suite 3
Eugene, OR 97401

www.wipfandstock.com

PAPERBACK ISBN: 978-1-5326-3220-4
HARDCOVER ISBN: 978-1-5326-3222-8
EBOOK ISBN: 978-1-5326-3221-1

Cataloguing-in-Publication data:

Names: Lingenfelter, Sherwood G.
Title: Leadership in the way of the cross : forging ministry from the crucible of crisis / Sherwood G. Lingenfelter.
Description: Eugene, OR: Cascade Books, 2018 | Includes bibliographical references.
Identifiers: ISBN 978-1-5326-3220-4 (paperback) | ISBN 978-1-5326-3222-8 (hardcover) | ISBN 978-1-5326-3221-1 (ebook)
Subjects: LCSH: Leadership. | Organizational effectiveness. | Vulnerability (personality trait). | Success—Religious aspects—Christianity.
Classification: BV45983.3 .L565 2018 (print) | BV45983 (ebook)

MAY 7, 2018

Dedication

To the one hundred twenty-nine men and women enrolled in the doctor of ministry program at Alliance Theological Seminary, Nyack, NY, from 2011 to 2016, who processed with me, and with one another, their stories of leadership crisis. While we shared together some of the most painful moments in our ministry lives, out of our times of group reflection—Scripture, prayer, and processing openly our ministry failures—we discovered the joy of loving one another, of unity in the body of Christ, and of experiencing healing, restoration, and renewal in our respective callings as servants of the Lord Jesus Christ. With special gratitude to those who gave permission to share in this book personal reflections of your journey through crisis to flourishing—to God be the glory!

Contents

List of Tables and Figures

Preface

In the winter of 2008, the global financial crises hit every sector of the US economy. Fuller Theological Seminary was no exception. As the provost and chief operating officer at Fuller, I returned from a sabbatical in January of 2009 to face the challenge of leading the people of the seminary through the unfamiliar and hostile terrain of economic crisis. I had no road map, blueprint, or proven leadership solution for this crisis. However, in the months preceding that time, God had opened my eyes to new principles of leadership through reflection on a prior leadership crisis with twenty international Christian leaders from around the world. This book tells the story of that deep reflection and learning how to forge new paths for leadership from these crises.

The joy of a sabbatical is that it provides time for reading, reflection and exploring new things. Shortly before our leave, my wife, Judy, a PhD in anthropology and education, had been invited to review for *Christian Education Journal* the book *Leadership Can Be Taught*, by Sharon Daloz Parks. Parks's book is the result of a five-year research project on the educational effectiveness of a class on leadership at Harvard's Kennedy School of Government taught by Ronald Heifetz. After preparing the review, Judy said to me, "Sherwood you must read this book." Being busy as provost at Fuller, I put it on my sabbatical "to read" list.

Providentially, we had been invited by Jonathan Bonk to spend the Fall 2008 semester as scholars in residence at the Overseas Ministry Study Center in New Haven, Connecticut. In our early sabbatical weeks we together read and discussed the works of Parks, Ronald Heifetz, and Heifetz and Martin Linsky. These books provoked us to think about new ways of teaching and learning about leadership. One of the distinctive aspects of

Heifetz's method is that every student in his class is required to submit a short case study of a personal leadership crisis, and process it with peers during the semester of the course. We concluded that the methods used at Harvard could be adapted to Christian leadership training and we took up the challenge to experiment with Heifetz's ideas ourselves.

Later that fall, as scholars in residence, we had the responsibility and opportunity to conduct a seminar for international church leaders from Nigeria, Uganda, Madagascar, Palestine, India, Indonesia, Burma, and Korea who were also in residence that year. The critically new component of this seminar was my invitation to them to process with me a crisis story of my leadership as provost at Biola University in 1998. I presented the case in written and oral formats, and we divided the participants into four groups of five, and asked them to reflect together on two questions about my case:

1. What false assumptions did I make? and

2. What opportunities did I miss?

I was absolutely stunned at the insights that I gained from these men and women on my case study. As they presented their group reflections on my questions and debriefed with me, I pondered why I had not sought this kind of consultation during the time of my crisis in 1998. I realized that my failure in large part was due to my default assumptions and behaviors about how to lead, and thus failing to utilize the people resources around me to meet the incredibly difficult challenges I was facing. This exercise opened a whole new line of thinking for me about how I would approach future leadership challenges and how I might teach leadership.

This one-week experimental seminar was a very significant moment in our learning about leadership and leadership training. We asked the Lord to guide us in how we might make this a future contribution in our ministry together. However, when I returned to Fuller after my sabbatical, I walked into the middle of the seminary financial crisis of 2009. So before I began to imagine what it would be like to teach these principles, I was forced to apply them and to put them into practice in my leadership at Fuller.

Later in the spring of 2010, leaders at Alliance Theological Seminary in Nyack, New York, invited both Judy and me to teach a course in their new doctor of ministry program. After reflecting on this opportunity, we agreed to accept the invitation. Judy and I together created what we believe is a distinctive doctor of ministry course that requires deep reflection and learning from one's personal case study of crisis in ministry. Most leaders who enrolled in the Alliance DMin program had no interest in revisiting some of the most painful days in their ministries. Some openly resisted, while others saw it as an opportunity to learn and were eager to go forward. Among ten cohorts over five years, nearly all came through the process gaining significant new insights into their leadership, and reenvisioning who they are as leaders and how they intend to lead their congregations in the coming years.

Acknowledgments

I am deeply indebted to Martin Sanders and the church and mission leaders in the doctor of ministry program at Alliance Theological Seminary who have endorsed the writing of this book and have given me permission to analyze the data from ten cohorts of doctoral students in this work. I am especially grateful to the many leaders who have given permission to quote from their seminar papers that reflect on their leadership crises. I am also grateful to ten cross-cultural mission leaders enrolled in the doctor of missiology program at Fuller Theological Seminary who studied with Judy and me, several of whom have given me permission to quote from their work in this book. I thank ATS students in the D110 cohort who read and critiqued an earlier version of this work, and from their feedback I have made substantive revisions. I am also grateful to Rev. Brent Haggerty and the Stonecrest Community Church for the opportunity to present materials in chapters 8–12 to their church board, staff, and lay leaders in a workshop in February 2016.

I am also grateful to many friends and colleagues who have read one of the many drafts of this book, and offered their insights about how I might revise and improve these earlier drafts. Among these I am especially indebted to my wife, Judith, who read and critiqued all versions, my son, Joel, Jim Kinney, Bill and Barb Schuit, Harold Dollar, Kurt Frederickson, Peter Lin, Anita Koeshall, Scott Sunquist, and Siew Pik Lim. They have reinforced my belief that when we work with and in accountability to the body of Christ, our offerings to our Lord are of greater value.

Introduction

After serving for a total of twenty-five years in senior leadership at Biola University and at Fuller Theological Seminary, I have had many leadership crises. For most of these crisis, I did the best job that I could at the time, buried the rubble left behind, and moved on. But in that definitive sabbatical moment in 2008, I discovered that intentional reflection on crisis produces powerful learning that is invaluable for future leadership. In this light, I begin this book with reflection on my first leadership crisis at Biola University in 1988.

I came to Biola University in 1983 as professor of anthropology to teach, write, and to support the dean of the new School of Intercultural Studies in the development of masters and doctoral programs for Christian mission. I had completed my PhD dissertation on the anthropological study of political leadership on a small island in Micronesia, and had taught courses in political anthropology. Christian leadership was not on my horizon at that time, until I served as outside reader for Bobby Clinton's PhD dissertation on Christian leadership at Fuller. Looking around me at Biola, I realized that I was the only one on the intercultural studies faculty with the relevant research experience to pick up this topic. And so, I began my research and reflection on Christian leadership.

In 1988 my dean, Marvin K. Mayers, surprised me, telling President Cook that I had excellent administrative gifts and the spiritual qualifications to serve him and the university as the provost and senior vice president. My journey into the provost office was a personal struggle about leaving my faculty position that I will not detail here, except to say I did not seek this office. In the late spring of 1988, Clyde Cook appointed me as the provost and senior vice president of Biola University, and thereby I began a twenty-five-year journey serving under two presidents as the number two leader in both a Christian university and a theological seminary.

My first leadership crisis occurred three weeks after I moved into the provost's office. One of the four deans who reported to me came asking for help. As I listened to his story of a conflict between a department chair and a senior faculty member, I remember thinking—this is why the faculty complained about the previous provost; the provost gets all the difficult decisions. And that is why I did not want this job.

After listening to the dean, I proposed a possible solution to the problem, and sent him back to the department chair. The next day he returned again and reported that the chair was adamant, my proposal was unacceptable, and further, the only solution was to suspend the faculty member from teaching in the fall semester. At that point, I suggested that the three of us meet in my office to discuss this matter face to face.

As we gathered for that meeting, I remembered my anthropology lectures about how the leader gains and maintains support in an organization. The best course of action is to satisfy the demands of followers if at all possible; if that doesn't work, then the next step is to influence them that an alternative course is in their best interest; and if that doesn't work, use persuasion so as to change their beliefs or attitudes about the question. If all of the above fails, then you may be required to use force to gain compliance. After listening to the department chair explain the details of the case, and why I should support a decision to suspend the senior faculty member from teaching, which I was not willing to do, I suggested some possible alternatives, and described what I felt were real benefits to the department, the university, and the faculty member. After listening to me, the chair responded, "I will only do this if you force me to do it. I believe it is absolutely the wrong solution, and the only course of action that is good for the students and the university is to suspend the faculty member."

It is important to say at this juncture that the chair's concern was not about a moral or an integrity issue, but rather about teaching methods and the chair's assessment of the quality of the faculty member's performance. The dean agreed with me that suspension could have possible legal consequence and provoke a severe reaction among other faculty in the university; that is why he came to me for help. I had now experienced firsthand the hard-line position of the department chair, and my four choices had been reduced to one, force. I sent them both away to take a couple of days to pray about this, seeking a better solution from the Lord.

In the meantime, I went to the president, and briefed him on the case, asking for advice. He reminded me that my job was to protect the president's office from these kinds of conflicts; he stated that the decision was mine, and my responsibility was to protect the university from poor decisions that could provoke unwarranted public controversy and legal action by its employees.

In two days, I met again with the dean, and asked if he had good news. As I expected, his message was the same; the department chair was adamant—only if forced! The dean pressed me with urgency, "Classes start in two weeks, and we need to get this done." So, under this pressure, I made the decision—you must give this faculty member a teaching assignment for the fall semester.

Was this a bad decision? Not for the senior faculty member, not for the university, and not for the dean, but my decision undermined the integrity, usurped the authority, and alienated the department chair. By using force, I lost forever that chair's support for any and all of my initiatives, and more damaging, I lost the support of other faculty in that department for the next eleven years of my tenure as provost. In retrospect, I clearly see this as my first leadership crisis and failure as the provost of Biola University.

Reality Check: Leadership—No Easy Answers

If I imagined that being provost might be an easy job, or one for which I was adequately prepared, this small crisis was my initiation by fire. As I look back thirty years, I can see now my false assumptions, my simplistic reliance upon a few theoretical principles, my default habits, and a pattern of leadership which today seems terribly immature and foolish. Yet at the time, I was reasonably certain that I was doing my job well.

Having served for five years on the Biola faculty, I had carefully studied the culture of the organization and community. I had learned to respect and work within its authority structures. I understood and supported the deep commitment of the leaders and the faculty to the authority of Scripture, to integrating Christian faith into a liberal education, and into the daily work of teaching and administration in the university. Coming to Biola after fifteen years in the SUNY university system, these faith commitments were invigorating. God's calling brought us to Biola from SUNY, enriched Judy and me with new opportunities for teaching, scholarship, and service.

My dean discerned my gifts accurately. God has blessed me with skills and experience for understanding organizations. I have the capacity to process and make sense of large quantities of information, and to use that data to make meaningful decisions, including writing books like this one. I love the work of listening to people, learning from their stories and experiences, and working with them to achieve common goals, and I have been rewarded for my effectiveness in this many times.

Further, I find joy in using my administrative leadership gifts to serve others. This flows naturally from who I am; I love tackling problems, exploring possible solutions, and testing these possibilities against the realities of the situation. I enjoy collaborative work with colleagues, brainstorming together about our opportunities and challenges, and I find great satisfaction in deep reflection that leads to constructive and innovative responses to such challenges.

Yet, to this day I have never sought a position of leadership, but rather have been asked to serve in these capacities by others with whom I have worked. Working from background supporting roles gave me the satisfaction of using my gifts to help others, without the pain and frustrations that those in top leadership positions endured. Often, I had resisted accepting formal leadership roles, perhaps because of how I have seen others suffer when they did so. The provost who served before me at Biola suffered much criticism and even hostility within the Biola community, so I knew that this was not a happy job.

Spiritually, I was convinced that God had led the president, the search committee, and the faculty to support my appointment; they were fully aware of my reluctance and my past history of rebellion and agnosticism on matters of faith. At that point in my life these matters were behind me, and I was and remain very much aware of the cost and joy of following Jesus Christ. I had memorized and internalized Jesus' words recorded in the gospels, "Whoever wants to be my disciple must deny themselves and take up their cross daily and follow me. For whoever wants to save their life will lose it, but whoever loses their life for me will save it" (Luke 9:23–24). I walked into the provost job with both a sense of death to a faculty life that I had loved, and discovery on the journey ahead with Jesus as I sought to follow him.

Three weeks into the job, I found that this was indeed going to be a difficult journey. I don't mind tough jobs, but my wife will tell you that my least favorite thing is cleaning out the garbage disposal in the kitchen that is plugged with potato peelings on a night when I arrive home from a long trip. The challenge of the conflict between a department chair and a senior faculty member was equivalent to Judy's plugged garbage disposal. The pressure to get the drain unplugged is high; the task involves unexpected resistance due to rust, location, and inadequate tools; and when the drain is opened, the garbage and water that runs out floods beneath the sink and onto the kitchen floor and onto me. Worse, unlike the water and garbage on the kitchen floor, the damage of my inept work in conflict resolution spread throughout the department into the university, and stained some relationships for years to come.

So What Are the Answers?

After more than two decades in academic leadership, service on two international mission boards, and more than one significant crisis, I am convinced that any leader who says "I have not failed" is either living in denial, or has occupied a position of leadership without ever taking the risk of leading. Genuine leadership is always about stepping up in crisis, facing the demands of people struggling with complex and difficult issues, and taking the risk of exercising leadership in the midst of opposition and threat. As I found in that first crisis, exercising leadership has little or nothing to do with the position one holds, and everything to do with learning how to work with people in difficult and challenging circumstances. My strategies—asking people to pray, hoping God will step in and change hearts, encouraging people to consider other options, delaying for a few days, trying to persuade one whose values and interests conflicted with mine—were utterly inadequate for that challenge. I had the position, I exercised the authority of that position, and I made a decision that resolved the crisis, but I did not lead. At the end of the day, I was managing effectively, but not leading. I applied a temporary patch to the crisis and the senior professor had a teaching assignment; but the crisis festered and the wounds bled for years to come.

What is the difference between managing and leading? Bob Davids declares that management is about control and is encumbered by the "triple constraint of management, the control of quality, time and money."[1] In my case the department chair was concerned about the quality of teaching, the

1. Davids, "The Rarest Commodity Is Leadership without Ego," TEDx Talk (video, 12:50), https://www.youtube.com/watch?v=UQrPVmcgJJk.

dean was concerned about the semester schedule (time), and about how to use a senior faculty member who had to be paid (money). We were all focused on management issues. Davids argues that leadership is not about management, it is about people. Where were the people in this crisis and how did I lead them? As I look back, I missed that challenge, and settled for a management decision that gave priority to time and money over the quality question raised by the department chair.

As I reflect on my career in academic and mission leadership, I have been an exceptional manager, but I have often been less effective in leading people. In my first crisis, no one followed me! Those who got what they wanted followed their prior ways, and those who were disappointed rejected me outright. No one was following; rather everyone did what was right in his/her own eyes. How might I have led so that people would have seen Jesus in me, and followed him?

Leading with Authority and Vulnerability

This book is for people who are serious about leading people—men and women who have accepted big challenges, who have passed through the fire of tough decisions, who have acknowledged they at times have failed, and have recovered for the next challenge, but do not want to repeat the past. However, I warn you before you read any further that I do not have three steps that you can take to keep from failing again. After multiple crises in my leadership lifetime, I can tell you that my leadership success and failure is rooted in who I am, in how my family has influenced me, in how God has equipped me, in how I have exercised his gifts, and how I bring all of this to the next crisis. You have a different calling and set of gifts, a distinctive family and life history, and you have led in places where I have not gone. Therefore, I cannot provide easy answers for you or for anyone else.

This book is about leading through what Andy Crouch has termed "authority and vulnerability"[2]—authority is a shared reality, embedded in the roles and power given to us by the people that we serve, and vulnerability is "exposure to meaningful risk"[3] that is inherent to the exercise of that authority in our service to God and to God's people. As Christians leaders,

2. Crouch, *Strong and Weak*, 4.

3. Vulnerability for Crouch, and in this book, is always used with reference to "exposure to meaningful risk," rather than to "emotional transparency," which is the more common reference. See ibid., 29–32.

we very often fear the seduction of authority or we hide from the pains that exposure to meaningful risk entail. Crouch argues that the journey of leadership is one that takes us deep into the dangers of both authority and vulnerability, and that our attempts to avoid one or the other of these dangers will precipitate crisis. To flourish, in contrast, is to embrace each in a manner that emulates the life and ministry of our Lord Jesus Christ.

As a leader who desires to flourish, I must always ask, "Is anyone following?" And are we following Jesus as we invite others to follow us? How important are the people to us, and do they have confidence and trust to follow? In the chapters to come, I am inviting you into my journey, and the journeys of others, into the deep waters of embracing our authority and the significant meaningful risks that made us vulnerable to crisis and failure of leading people. This process begins with self-discovery—disclosing default habits, fears and hungers—followed by trusting the Holy Spirit to work God's transformation within us, and then to engaging the hard work of mobilizing his body, the people of God, so that every part is doing his work.

A Brief Overview

Lee Ellis who endured years as a prisoner of war in Vietnam, assures us that effective leadership is forged in the crucible of our struggles.[4] The overall objective of this book is to provide a window through which Christian leaders may examine and process the threats, secrets and riches of their leadership crises.

Organized in four parts, the first part focuses on how leaders distort God's gift of authority and vulnerability, building from cases of brothers and sisters struggling with leadership crises. In part two we examine, through reflection on those struggles, how to confront our habits, fears and hungers and how to refocus our use of authority and vulnerability in such a way as to flourish as servants of the Lord Jesus Christ. Once we have understood both the distortions and proper use of authority and vulnerability, parts three and four point to how we may rethink our leadership as enabling Christ's body to do its work and embrace the authority and vulnerability of who we are in Christ to mobilize and empower God's people for God's mission.

---

4. Ellis, *Leading with Honor*, Kindle loc. 4720.

Part 1: Distortions of Authority and Vulnerability in Crisis

Reflections on crises expose the different layers of how we exercise authority and vulnerability, like a chef peels an onion. So, in chapter 1 we first look at the layer of default habits, such as those in my case study, that lead us down the pathway of management when leadership is needed. In chapter 2 we look at the deeper layer of emotions, such as fear of failure and shame, and the destructive impact of false assumptions about the thinking and motives of other people, that may lead us to withdrawal or even self-destruction.

In chapter 3 we examine the core layer of our character, and the effects of personal hungers for significance, power, intimacy, and the seduction of greed, that often blind us in our crises, so that we ignore critical data, and misuse authority and control to solve problems that actually required new learning on our part, and collaboration with others. Finally, in chapter 4 we analyze how the use and misuse of authority and power to avoid risk is so frequently at the core of leadership crisis and oftentimes failure.

Part 2: Recovering the Paradox—Embracing Vulnerability

Christ's way of leading is both authoritative as our master and vulnerable as our servant. Chapter 5 presents the first step of embracing this paradox—exposing the "termites of self" that undermine leadership to the refining light and fire of the Holy Spirit. Chapter 6 shifts focus to learning to embrace Christ's balance of authority and vulnerability, through the interplay of four spiritual disciplines, and celebrating God's work of change through gratitude and worship. Chapter 7 invites the reader to replace habits of command/control with practices of leadership that blend both authority and vulnerability—the way of the cross, so as to imitate Christ and give Glory to God. Such strategies of leadership embrace learning and empower people to do adaptive, spirit-focused work in times of crisis.

Part 3: Building a Christ-Centered Culture of Flourishing

Crises expose our vulnerabilities. Crises provide opportunities to lead like Christ. Ephesians 2:14–22 declares that we are Christ's body, a spiritual house in which God dwells, a house that embraces Jew and Gentile, diverse yet one. So, our next question is what are the structural pillars in each Christ-centered culture of flourishing? Chapters 8 and 9 explore the two corner posts essential for every cultural expression of this spiritual house: the first is an all-consuming focus to glorify God in every work of love and obedience, and the second is embracing the fundamental truth that all ministry is body work done in one Spirit, one Lord, and one baptism, with each diverse manifestation of the spiritual house an expression of the "body of Christ."

Chapters 10, 11 and 12 propose three pairs of supporting pillars that express the presence of Christ in the working relationships of each cultural expression of his body, a spiritual house in which God dwells. Each of these structural pairs exhibit the authority and vulnerability of our Lord Jesus Christ: his word is our source of authority and his weakness—the way of the cross—defines our pathway of leadership; our practices of fellowship and forgiveness create essential bonds of unity among us; and our obedience in worship and witness enable us to fulfill God's mission for his church and to stand against the attacks of spiritual and human opposition. Each is counterintuitive to our normal cultural habits and ministry practices, yet each leads us deeper into the essence of who we are as the servants of the Lord Jesus Christ.

Chapter 13 concludes this part with a recap of the core issues of authority and vulnerability in Christ. We are clearly human, formed wonderfully by our creator; but at the same time flawed, weak, wounded and broken, in the words of the Apostle Paul, "clay pots." How does God work in us when we face crisis and even failure with the intent to be transformed in our vulnerability and conformed in our authority to the image of Christ?

Part 4: Going Further?

Part 4 is a postscript that presents specific opportunities for the reader to apply the windows into self and the biblical principles presented throughout the book in their practice of ministry. Chapter 14 provides a brief definition of the "case-in-point" process, created by Ronald Heifetz,[5] and then practical exercises for reflection, writing, and peer review that will lead to the exposure of the "termites" that undermine one's leadership. Chapter 15 concludes the book with two reflective, and very practical means for turning leadership crises into a rehearsal for godly leadership.

I confess to the reader that I did not embark on this journey of self-reflection on my crucible of leadership crises until 2008 at the age of

5. Parks, *Leadership Can Be Taught*, 6.

sixty-seven, twenty years after I accepted the invitation to serve as the senior vice president at Biola University. In retrospect, I wonder how much more effective I could have been if I had discovered how to learn from these struggles at age forty-seven, after my first leadership crisis at Biola. As I look back over those twenty years, many things went well, but I also recall crises in which I did not lead well. I remember the many hours spent in prayer and anguish about those crises, pondering how I could have been more effective as a servant of the Lord Jesus Christ.

I know now, after my deep reflection on that sabbatical in 2008, that I did become a more effective leader at Fuller until I retired in 2011. My colleagues will testify that my leadership was less than perfect, but I did finish reasonably well. But how I wish I had learned these lessons at a younger age. That is why I am writing this book, with the hope and joy that when you discover these principles and apply them to your leadership, the Holy Spirit will lead you into deeper self-reflection on how you lead, and enable you to grow and flourish into all that God has in mind for you as a shepherd of his flock in his global church. The more than one hundred men and women who have taken this journey with us at Alliance Theological Seminary have found it a journey that brings invigorating hope, significant new direction and change in their practice of leadership, and flourishing as they experience the joy and work of the Holy Spirit in the body of Christ.

Part One

DISTORTIONS OF AUTHORITY AND VULNERABILITY IN CRISIS

1

Default Habits and Missing God's Priorities

Michael pastors a Reformed church in a small, suburban town in northern New Jersey. The church is predominantly white, Dutch, mostly middle class and "blue collar." It is theologically evangelical, conservative and the polity is Presbyterian, with annually elected deacons and elders to serve on the consistory. Though the congregation elects people to serve, they do not always appear to trust those elected. Church polity places decision-making powers in the hands of the consistory (similar to any representative government). The consistory has the right to make many decisions about personnel and operations without a general vote of every member, though for decisions to call a minister of word and sacrament (and large financial decisions), congregational approval has been generally sought.

At a 2013 consistory meeting, Michael noted that they decided to change the assistant pastor's status from part-time to full-time without calling a congregational meeting. Their reasoning behind their action was that the position in question was a staff contract, not an official ministry call, and therefore they acted within the bounds of their authority and their overall budget.

Over the next few weeks they heard rumblings that a congregational meeting should have been held. And, as so often happens, their action also surfaced other issues and resentments that people had. Some accused the consistory of an almost conspiratorial action—leading out of an agenda to redirect the church according to the plans of a few. Over the next few months, certain people were noticeably absent or infrequent in their attendance on Sunday morning. Obvious issues of trust, power, and control were at work on both sides.

Michael expressed surprise and commented that it seemed like much ado about nothing. He confessed to becoming a bit angry and resentful. In his opinion, the consistory clearly acted in the right and the opposition did not have a leg to stand on. He dismissed these grumblings as from those who simply did not adequately understand church polity; they belonged to a Reformed church, but wanted to function like a congregational church; they elected people to lead, but then resented them when they actually did so. Frustrated by the fact that they, as leaders, sought to move ahead in faith, while others resisted and caused problems, he declared, "I wanted to be efficient and effective and make something happen."[1]

Michael's case is one of 129 stories of leadership crisis that men and women, serving in full-time church and mission ministries, have shared with me, and with one another, about their leadership crises. They have come from a wide diversity of cultures, denominations and leadership positions. They have had rich experiences and success in leadership in urban, suburban, and global ministry contexts. At the same time, they all have experienced crises in which things have not turned out as they had wished, and in some cases severely impacted their lives and effectiveness. In this chapter I will share some of what we have learned together about ministry focus and our default habits of leadership.

Leading People or Managing Routine Problems?

Michael and I share a common ministry focus. As I reflect on my leadership failure in 1988, I interpreted the department chair crisis as part of the "dirty work" of the provost office; I remembered how people had complained about the previous provost, and so now it would be me. In a similar way, Michael saw the decision to change a pastor's status as part of the routine work of the consistory. He was surprised at the complaints that arose from this decision, and frustrated that people were upset. He too became angry

---

1. Michael's story and the others that follow—written as part of their participation in the author's leadership skills course in the doctor of ministry program at Alliance Theological Seminary—have been included in this volume by written permissions granted to the author.

and resentful about "much ado about nothing." We both wanted to be efficient, effective, and make something happen.

As I look back it is clear to me now that Michael and I made assumptions about the people—they became problems to be solved. We silently questioned their spiritual commitment, and openly asked them to pray in hopes that God will help them see how foolishly they were behaving. Blaming the people—stubborn, inept, critical, uncooperative, unreasonable—is a way of avoiding the leadership challenge. I needed a solution that would avoid risk, satisfy as many as possible, and allow us to move on to the more important work of the university. Nothing in my imagination at that time would have prompted me to ask, "What is God doing in this crisis, and how can I be the servant who will bring glory to his name?"

Over the past five years I have read more than one hundred case studies of ministry failure, and these stories are much the same. Pastor Jeff needs someone to lead the Christian Education ministry; Pastor Doug is concentrating on a quality worship experience on Sunday morning, and struggling to get the musicians to rehearse and work together. Bishop Carlton is called to put out a fire of broken relationships among African American women providing food for the poor in the inner city. Mission leader Joanna has a vision to train Mali women leaders for inductive Bible studies. Pastor Lezlie is called to arbitrate a dispute among women about whether or not to continue the Sunday morning coffee hour. Pastor Mark, a district leader, is given the task to deploy a young leader to revitalize a church. Assistant Pastor Sandra writes a curriculum to deal with inappropriate sexual behavior within a worship team.

In every case the leader faced a specific task or relational issue in their ministry context, and defined that issue as a people problem to be solved. Each of the leaders, trained for ministry, carefully looked through their knowledge, skills, and experience in ministry and acted to "get it done." In each of these cases, the leader chose a course of action that led to pain, more broken relationships, and a sense of personal failure about their ministry to others.

What I have learned from our collective crises is that we must first do the hard work of examining ourselves to surface the habitual motivations and patterns of response we typically employ in a crisis. Once our eyes are open to discern our own habits and motivations, we may then ask what God's purpose may have been for each crisis, and what God may want us to accomplish through such challenges. Self-discovery only happens by the periodic, continuing work of deep reflection; perhaps this is part of what Jesus meant by taking up our cross daily.

In the rest of this chapter I will explore three areas for reflection about typical default habits of American pastors and missionaries that surface when we are facing crisis: first, a "performance-driven" culture of leadership, second, undisclosed values conflicts, and third, a reliance upon command/control actions that we employ to solve problems. Once we have surfaced these issues in our leadership practices, we have the capacity to reframe the problem and define the end goal so as to see more clearly new opportunities for obedience to our Lord.

Exposing Our "Performance-Driven" Goals

In the United States of America, we live in a culture driven by values for achievement and quick, short-term solutions to problems. Immigrants see this, and if they want to survive, they adopt these values, or cultivate them if they shared similar values when they came. Congregations expect a polished performance in preaching and worship; and they expect excellence in the diverse programs of the church. As a consequence of these high expectations, most church and mission leaders in the United States, regardless of ethnicity and race, give highest priority to excellent, on-time ministry performance.

Michael, in the Reformed church case study, notes his motivation for quick, efficient, and effective decision-making. I have termed this *task-focused leadership* that requires equipping and leading others in the task-focused social game of the particular ministry in question.[2] In Michael's case, the consistory was charged with the task, and took appropriate action. As a member of the consistory, Michael and the others reasoned together that this decision was within their authority, and required no further consultation. When the crisis erupted, they were surprised, yet they knew and acknowledged the "congregational" governance leanings of their people.

In the variety of ministry team crises and failures that we have processed with other pastors, these leaders have all experienced value conflicts with volunteers, and in their distress, they have defaulted to old habits of dealing with crisis. For some, that might be trying practice-oriented solutions, for others the use of power to correct the situation, and for still others, denial, hoping that the situation will change, until the crisis overwhelms

2. Lingenfelter, *Leading Cross-Culturally*, 70.

the team. All of them missed the opportunity to see their team in crisis as an opportunity to help participants become more mature followers of Jesus. Why is this so? My contention is that they, like me, often see people as problems to be solved, and they work from "performance-driven" goals.

Value Conflicts That Compound Vulnerability

Performance pressure in crises usually is compounded by the undercurrent of divergent values between different parties. All crisis situations in ministry have inherent within them value conflict, yet people rarely take the time, or perhaps have a reflective moment to probe underneath the surface to discern the value issues at stake.

To illustrate, I have presented in table 1.1 my reflection in 2015 upon the value conflicts between the department chair and the dean in 1988, as I remember listening to their complaints and their fears. However, if I had openly asked them to articulate their values in 1988, I would have learned much more. I also could have sought advice from some of their colleagues who had worked with them on other occasions for other purposes. The point here is that the values of others are usually not disclosed openly, but surface indirectly through public exchanges of anger, fear, or resistance to something the leader has said or done. In some cases, our friends try to give us advice, but if we did not ask for it, it is very hard for us to take seriously what is said.

As I look back at this case in table 1.1, using a basic values framework,[3] it is clear that the dean and the department chair had significant expectations and values that were in conflict—the chair focused on task, while the dean focused on the person; the chair insisted that this was a crisis requiring immediate intervention, the dean's perspective was non-crisis, hoping to manage this issue over time; the chair demanded curricular alignment, while the dean preferred flexibility in management. At the same time, they have enough in common—concern for integrity, quality, and competence—that a potential existed for collaboration together. If I had explored this further by seeking the advice of their peers and colleagues, I might have approached the crisis in a very different way.

---

3. Lingenfelter and Mayers, *Ministering Cross-Culturally*, 18–19.

TABLE 1.1 Value Conflicts in the Senior Faculty Crisis	
Department Chair's Values	*Dean's Values*
Excellence in teaching Satisfaction among students	Competent teaching, diversity Quality education
Integrity of department Curricular alignment	Institutional integrity Flexibility in management
Task, individual responsibility Crisis, correction of situation	Person, loyalty to colleagues Non-crisis, together over time
Time—semester deadline "Incompetence" must be addressed	Time—semester deadline Can we work together to resolve?

Why did I miss all this in 1988? I confess that my time alone with God was spent complaining about the difficult people God had brought into my life, and asking God to do something about it. This was not productive, most of all because I was trying to avoid the pain, and I did not think to ask what God was doing and how I might partner with him. In retrospect, I wish I had used my quiet time for deep reflection, asking questions about the different values that motivated me and others, and about God's mission for that situation.

Once we have surfaced what we believe are reasonably accurate accounts of undisclosed values, we may be ready to process together what we have learned. On what points do we share common values, or at least values that we can respect and accept as members of the body of Christ? What seem to be the value differences that are driving the conflict? What is my responsibility as God's servant in this case? This is the place to begin our prayers, seeking God's purpose and some clarity in our next steps.

Command/Control to Avoid Vulnerability

The next step in self-examination is more difficult, and few of us have the ability to surface default leadership habits alone. Heifetz and Linsky help us with their discussion of the habits of most leaders to seek quick and ready solutions for problems (they call this "technical work").[4] Kevin Ford suggests that this habit stems from our assumption that "leadership is a noun" and that we understand leading as either using power to make things

---

4. Heifetz and Linsky, *Leadership on the Line*, 14.

happen, or exercising authority to satisfy those we serve.[5] Leaders who exercise "command and control" have, in fact, a virtual toolbox of technical solutions for problems, and their default behavior is to go to that box. In the case of the senior faculty member, I took the last of four solutions in my toolbox, and I forced the department chair to schedule a teaching assignment. This worked in the short term, but damaged all working relationships among the four of us for the long term. Each of the men and women whose cases I briefly cited above will tell you that their first responses, technical solutions, also did not work, and the suffering and pain that followed exceeded the benefit of "quick and ready" solutions.

Once again it is helpful to probe more deeply. In your quiet time alone with God, make a list of what you see as your "default settings" in crisis. If you use a cultural values assessment tool, you could assess your personal value profile and ask, which of these values become the "deciding value," overriding everything else for you in a situation of crisis?[6] In table 1.2 you will see that all three of these academic leaders (provost, dean, and department chair) had the same flawed view and default habits of leadership—get it done, apply a technical solution, make authority-driven decisions. Michael, in the Reformed church case study that opened the chapter, followed that exact same strategy. Heifetz suggests that we all have a truncated view of leadership, relying on authority alone, and technical solutions to resolve issues that require learning, and adaptive change.[7]

TABLE 1.2 Default "Command/Control Settings" in the Senior Faculty Crisis	
Lingenfelter/Dean Defaults	*Department Chair Default*
University trumps department interest	Department integrity trumps faculty tenure
Time—get it done Technical solution—force teaching role	Time—get it done Technical solution—no teaching role
It's my job, my authority Lingenfelter must solve!	It's my job, my authority Only if you force me!

5. Ford, *Transforming Church*, 94–95.

6. See Lingenfelter and Mayers, *Ministering Cross-Culturally*, Hofstede et al., *Cultures and Organizations*, or Plueddemann, *Leading across Cultures*, for value assessment tools.

7. Heifetz, *Leadership without Easy Answers*, 76.

Our challenge as leaders is to know ourselves, because in times of crisis we will not do God's will, we will default to strategies, values, and habits that have driven us in the past. Yes, Michael and the consistory have the formal authority and can provide biblical justification for their decision about the pastoral intern. Yes, the department chair and the provost can provide biblical justification for their positions on "individual responsibility" or "corporate commitment," but Jesus challenges us to discover our own shortcomings—to judge ourselves and then show mercy to others in proportion to the mercy we have received (Matt 7:1–5). And in retrospect, my job as leader was to make the space and time to process the value clashes in such a way that God would be glorified. Instead, I heard and ignored the value clashes, and defaulted to a technical solution in order to meet an institutional time deadline.

Reflection: Default Habits and Missing God's Priorities

The writer of Hebrews reminds us that our first priority is to "draw near to God" (Heb 10:22). As we have explored above, default habits and value conflicts distract us from the main thing. One leader, Joel, confessed, "When I move from stress to distress the following happens, . . . I work harder, . . . I take on doing the work by myself . . . and I stop praying for God to change me and help me lead well." When our relationship to God is weakened, or occasional, we depend more and more upon ourselves, and less upon God. So many of the leaders in our study have confessed that the intense workload of ministry has separated them from God, crushed their spiritual intimacy, and often left them in a barren spiritual wilderness.

Once separated from God, the second command, to "hold unswervingly to the hope we profess" (Heb 10:22), becomes an intellectual exercise in preparation for preaching and teaching, without the passion and joy that flows from an intimate walk with God. Having been trained well, we may still be effective in doing the work of ministry but the broken people that God brings to our congregations and to our teams make a mess of things, and we resort to command/control leadership. Bishop Carlton observes, "While approaching the challenge with a command control posture is the easy way out, oft times it represents the coward's way out in terms of our expressing the whole of the Christ mandate." Like the priests in Malachi (1:13), the work is hard and the people burdensome, and we are tempted to say as they did, "What a burden!" and we sniff at it contemptuously.

God's primary concern is not about our ministry performance, but about our being his covenant people, people who reflect this wonderful new identity we have, as people on a "new and living way" to God through the blood of Jesus Christ. Through the confidence we have in Jesus, we may then "draw near to God," hold fast to our hope in him, and "spur one another on toward love and good deeds." This latter task is the work of God's mission, which brings honor to his name, and through our obedience to him, establishes God's kingdom through his church.

The critical lesson for leaders is that the ministry—the offerings of sermons and worship services, or classes and instruction, or a food program for the poor—is *not* the main thing! Our relationship with God is the core of our calling, and we do ministry as a means to bring other people into a deeper relationship with God. When we do ministry for its own sake, it is idolatry. And God takes no pleasure in our offerings or our sacrifices; God's pleasure comes in people who do his will (Heb 10:7), and who bring awe and reverence to his name among the nations of the earth.

Therefore, since we are receiving a kingdom that cannot be shaken, let us be thankful, and so worship God acceptably with reverence and awe, for our "God is a consuming fire" (Heb 12:28–29).

Reflection Questions:

1. What expectations did Michael's congregation have that were not met?

2. In what actions was Michael driven by a performance mentality?

3. What do you think were the value conflicts between Michael and his congregation?

4. How did Michael use his command/control toolbox?

2

Distortions of Fear,
False Assumptions, and Judgment

Timothy, a second-generation Chinese church planter, had a vision for a multicultural church in suburban area near New York City. With a small group of friends and coworkers they achieved constant and healthy growth to about two hundred people in four years. Building upon a philosophy of equality among leaders and members, Timothy formed a church board with seven members of diverse origins that made consensus decisions about church direction, with occasional congregational voting to assure support for their decisions. Board members at times had sharp disagreements. A particularly intense moment came when Timothy presented a vision to begin a Chinese language ministry for recent immigrants. When they could not agree, Timothy chose to pray and delay, and to seek further direction from the congregation. Through hard work on Timothy's part, he was finally able to achieve enough consensus to start the immigrant ministry.

Later, a gift in the form of seven acres of land and a small retail building was offered to the church for its ministries. Members of the board had intense and personal arguments about how to discern God's will on this gift. After some weeks of prayer and waiting, Timothy led the board to a compromise solution to rent another church facility for worship (favored by Thorn, a strong voice on the board), and to utilize the several acres gift site, at minimal cost and maintenance, for community outreach (preferred by another strong board member, but opposed by Thorn). The congregation supported this compromise.

After several more months of prayer and discussion, Timothy put forth a four-step plan to deal with facility issues and add two more half-time pastors to meet the needs of the two growing congregations. The board approved the decision, but with one condition demanded by Thorn—approval from a general congregation meeting. A week after the congregation approved (83% positive), Thorn and his wife announced that God had called them to another church. When Timothy visited them to discern why, Thorn complained that Timothy used his executive power to overrule his and his wife's ministry goals. After this family departed, more than ten other families left the church. Timothy comments on how he managed these crises:

> I am willing and open to field discussion and suggestions from the significant people around me. I hope to find a common solution for the problem that fits all. Yet, when I unconsciously sense the risk of rejection and abandonment, the stress of resolving the problem becomes very high. I fall into finding a compromising solution and hope that there is a pathway to resolve the matter later.

Dark Fears That Distort Vulnerability

Fear is an emotion that exposes our vulnerability and leads us to actions that, in retrospect, we often regret. Timothy cites his fear of rejection and abandonment coupled with a board environment that prefers consensus, leading him to find compromise solutions on very complex and challenging matters in his ministry. These compromises gave him a pathway of hope, but in the long term really satisfied no one.

In a similar way, my decision to override the department chair and grant the dean's request was based as much upon fear as any other factor. So, what fears colored my thinking and decision process? I talked to the dean about what I perceived to be a very real threat of a public grievance by the senior faculty member or even a lawsuit. I quietly wondered if this was the beginning of bad press on the new provost; could it be that I, too, would be reviled by the faculty in a few years? Or, could it be that in this first major decision I might fail to protect the president from the very kinds of conflict and bad press that he had hired me to manage?

The truth is that all of the above surely were part of my thinking, and perhaps in a parallel way of Timothy's, as well. Timothy and I share an obsession—to do a job well. I learned this from my father, who learned it from his father. I expect that Timothy learned his obsession from his father. So then, what about the fear of not doing well? Is that a deeper, darker fear that we have not addressed? My pastor friend, Jeff, comments on this very issue:

> When we release control, we entrust others to act in ways that may not fit with our idea of how they should act. We take the risk that whatever task or responsibility we have released will not be done in accord with our design, and in the worst case, we are willing to accept failure on the part of others with all of its consequences. There it is, failure, my greatest nightmare. The dark side of an identity centered on competence is an inability to process, or even accept failure. I honestly fear failure more than I fear death.

In one group of ministry leaders we were coaching, ten out of ten agreed that fear was the most important emotional issue in their leadership crisis. For eight of those ten, that fear was the fear of failure itself, and for two of the ten, the fear of shame was even greater than the fear of failure. Shame is such a powerful emotion, and the dark side of fear or shame may drive a person to behaviors that lead to self-destruction. For example, a distinguished Chinese pastor committed adultery in a moment of weakness. When confronted by his board, and given an opportunity for repentance and restoration, his fear of shame drove him to reject his board, refuse both repentance and restoration, and then, defying his board, he split his church, taking those with him who either did not know, or supported his shame-avoidance. In all of this his fear of shame overcame his fear of the Lord, and made him impervious to the spiritual and emotional costs of broken relationships with his wife, family, and spiritual community that he had nurtured for more than a decade.

Dark fears and the denial of failure have serious emotional and spiritual consequences. As I have shared with you above, I wounded and marginalized the very people God had called me to love and to lead. Timothy wounded at least ten families in the fellowship of believers that he had loved and nurtured.

Jesus describes this as a fear of "losing one's life," or as Jeff describes it, losing an identity that is centered on competence. And as assuredly as we work harder to save our identity centered on competence and the works of ministry that confer that identity, we are destroying the covenant relationship with God and Christ that is the foundation of all that we are and do.

False Assumptions and the Misuse of Authority

I am ashamed to confess that it took me ten years of leadership before I began to ask the question: what false assumptions did I make that led me down this path? As human beings, we are so quick to make assumptions about situations and others, and we rarely stop to question those assumptions. This habit is pervasive, it colors all relationships—friends, family, workplace, and leadership. As Timothy, Michael, and I look back on our cases of conflict, we now see so many false assumptions, we wonder how we could have been so blind. However, let me detail a few, and suggest the consequences of them.

Assumptions about time limitations are one of the most common factors leading to bad decisions of church and mission leaders. When Timothy had the opportunity from his denomination to accept a gift of property for his church plant, board member Thorn objected and convinced others to follow him. Fearing that delay might result in the loss of this opportunity, Timothy pushed a compromise to accept the property for ministry and to rent another facility for worship. On the surface, this kind of time pressure is legitimate, and difficult to refute or reframe. Yet, as you already know, conceding this point created more financial and maintenance pressure for the congregation, and Thorn did not relent, forcing more compromises, and in the end, Thorn and other families left.

In my case, the dean first presented the crisis with reference to limited time. "The final registration for fall semester starts in two weeks; the faculty member does not have a course assignment; any later date, and students will miss the final registration opportunity." Once I accepted the time boundary, I drastically limited my capacity to lead. The other participants knew these same boundaries, and used work avoidance strategies to increase pressure on me for a technical decision. Allowing institutional deadlines to set the framework for complex issues that have long-term implications invariably leads to seriously flawed decisions. As I look back over years of academic leadership, I can count many decisions made under such time limitations that I regret.

One might ask, what options did I have? In retrospect I can imagine many options, but the real issue is how could I have exercised responsible leadership? My first responsibility as a leader is to use my authority to re-frame the time boundary. To allow fall registration to define the framework of such a significant and complex issue is to abdicate my authority to an institutional calendar, and to those who seek to use it to assert their author-ity on a complex issue. I could have redefined the time we would allocate to resolving these issues, but I did not even think to do so.

The second false assumption I made was about my role and respon-sibility. As I reflect back on this case study, I clearly assumed that I had to make this decision alone. Further, I assumed that the dean and others expected me to make the decision alone. In hindsight, my authority gave me many options. I could have gathered four or five other department chairpersons in the university, presented the situation to them, and asked them to give me good advice. Not only would that have been wise, most would have been honored by my request, asking for help. Further, if I had taken that initiative, I could have invited the chair with the crisis to present his case for denying the teaching assignment. Perhaps his colleagues would have been more successful than me to influence him to see this matter a bit differently. However, lacking this wisdom, I defaulted to my habit of acting alone.

Judging the Other and Marginalizing the Person

After listening to the department chair's ultimatum, "the only way I will do this is if you force me," I concluded that the department chair was a difficult person. The "difficult person" judgment is very common among leaders. Timothy found Thorn a difficult person, in spite of all of his efforts to collaborate with Thorn. When we experience a person who challenges our thinking on an issue, or rigorously resists a decision we have made, our inclination is to conclude that they are difficult people. This judgment allows us to relegate the person to a peripheral status. She or he is no longer worthy of our careful listening and discernment. We exclude such persons, judging their values suspect, their personalities difficult, and we work to carefully neutralize their influence and behavior.

Assigning the status "difficult person" not only marginalizes, it alien-ates the person and turns them into more hostile adversaries. While Thorn complained that Timothy used his executive power to overturn his and his wife's ministry goals, his deeper anger was about being marginalized in a series of ministry decisions. Sensing Timothy's rejection, he responded in kind, and from that point on all possible relationship was gone.

In my case, without even talking to the senior faculty member, I assumed from his prior work and relationships that he would respond aggressively if denied a teaching assignment. My assumptions and judgment created a communication gap between us that was of my own making. I was reluctant to explore with him alternatives because I assumed he had influence and power that he would use if my decision did not go his way. I also marginalized him in my decision process, and I was unfaithful to the Lord and to these two persons in our community of faith.

Instead of embracing the meaningful risks and doing the hard work of listening to both the department chair and the senior faculty, working to understand their values and hopes for the students they served, I took the easy path and made a technical decision. Instead of prayerfully creating time and space to bring the two together as members of one body, I used my power to force one to yield to the other. When the fall semester began, the senior faculty member was teaching, but all of the issues that were underneath this conflict remained unresolved. It is clear that my leadership did not bring glory to God, nor did it strengthen the university or bring resolution to complex issues.

We have heard similar stories from many pastors and missionaries about their leadership in congregations and mission organizations. We are all very busy people, feeling the pressure of limited time and the heavy load of work. When one person has the courage to challenge something we think is the right thing to do, what is our first response? Listen to Jeff's story:

> (Thinking) Wow, that's not what I heard from Judy or Jim. Why is Jane's take on Loretta so different from theirs? "Emotional stability?" You know, frankly, there are times that I question Jane's emotional stability. I'll talk to Roy. . . . If he gives me a "thumbs up," I'll know that this is just an interpersonal thing between Loretta and Jane, and I can't worry about our leaders trying to keep everybody happy.

We can sense from Jeff's words that he is under pressure, and feels he needs to make a decision soon (time pressure). After asking Jane for her advice, he rejects her counsel against his proposal, and marginalizes her as a person by questioning her emotional stability. Over time, Jane's counsel proves more reliable than the other advice Jeff received, but too late for Jeff. Jane senses Jeff's rejection and his withdrawal from her, and after a period of time she leaves his church. Jeff appoints Loretta to a ministry for which she is emotionally unprepared, and she, too, ends up leaving the church. Jeff and I share a common story: through our quick assumptions and "difficult person" judgments, we alienated our sisters and brothers in Christ, and we broke covenant with God to follow God's way.

Freedom from Fear, False Assumptions, Judgment

As I reflect back on these case studies, we (Timothy, Jeff, and I) grieve over our false assumptions, judgments, and default behaviors and the damage that resulted from them. But even more seriously, we violated our calling as servants of the Lord Jesus Christ, and our covenant relationship with God to do his will. This is not to say that we will not experience difficult people; such people are indeed certain when we step into leadership, and as we seek to collaborate with difficult people we will experience crises. The question is how will we respond.

Our challenge was and is to discover the delicate balance between our authority and our vulnerability; and act in the strength of our relationship in Christ. It is our vulnerability, knowing that in our own strength we cannot prevail and embracing meaningful risk, that empowers us to live the life of faith in the Christ who is our authority and strength. Fear undermines that balance. When we allow fear to overcome our faith, we are tempted to seek power and control to avoid risk. When we act out of fear, false assumptions and judgment follow quickly in that path.

Reflection on our stories of crisis enables us to surface the presence and reality of fear, and to experience the joy of transfiguration through God's mercy and grace as we let go of our own power and control, and rely once again on the power of the cross and the resurrection of our Lord Jesus Christ. In the practice of leadership, freedom comes when we remove the cloak of self-assurance that covers our false assumptions and disclose them in the light! Freedom follows confessing our sins of judgment and condemnation of the "difficult persons." Freedom confronts the false identity centered on competence with its dark fears of loss, and embraces the new identity centered on Jesus Christ that empowers us to take meaningful risk, knowing that there is no condemnation to those who are centered in him.

Reflection Questions:

1. What fears undermined Timothy's authority and vulnerability?

2. How did Timothy act to protect his vulnerability?

3. What opportunities to lead people did Timothy miss in this crisis?

3

Distortions of Hungers and Greed

John, missionary and team leader for a development ministry in the Middle East, had recruited and trained two men and two women as loyal and practiced national colleagues. John described his role as "leaderful leading," in which everyone was empowered to share ideas and all had voice. Success was clearly John's driving motivation for their development projects, and he believed that this passion was shared by the members of his team. Ideally, every voice was valued, but John was clearly the team leader, who as catalyst used his influence to motivate and empower the members of his team.

Under the pressure of budgets, tight deadlines, and creating systems for set-up and tear down for a specific public market project, John's team members disagreed with and resisted some of his decisions. When he refused to hear their voice, and supported an outside rival perspective, two team members disconnected with him (and the project), as wounded and denigrated partners. John responded with anger, hurt, and a sense of betrayal; further, he was embarrassed, believing that their resistance reflected poorly on him and might even destroy the reputation of the team if this project somehow fell short of his goals.

John states, "I became the high-power director of the project and treated the members of my team as employees. In my immense pride with being known for my accomplishments, my shadow mission for respect and notoriety took over, and I defaulted toward goal orientation." For John, the task, not the team, became his first priority. In his highly competitive drive to push through obstacles and red tape to get things done, he abandoned influence and used command/control to achieve success. His team stopped following and withdrew.

The Good, Bad, and Ugly of Hungers

Human hungers for power, importance, intimacy and for more of anything (greed) are so normal and pervasive that we rarely think about them. Most people aspire to do things that are significant, and we want and need the affirmation and acceptance of others. And, from infancy to old age we long to have intimate emotional and physical connections with others who are close to us.

The hunger for meaning and significance lies at the core of all human achievement, contributing to innovation, and economic and social change for thousands of years. People who have such hungers, like John in the story above, are often driven to do great things that contribute to church, mission and the wider society. John is clear that his hunger for success became a driving passion that enabled his team to achieve a very large public market project of significant benefit to many local vendors and to the whole urban community. My first point, then, is that human hungers are normal, common, and may potentially contribute much that is good.

However, Heifetz and Linsky write that these "normal hungers for power, importance and intimacy," if left unchecked, may lead to our self-destruction.

> Sometimes we bring ourselves down by forgetting to pay attention to ourselves. We get caught up in the cause and forget that exercising leadership is, at heart, a personal activity. It challenges us intellectually, emotionally, spiritually, and physically. But with the adrenaline pumping, we can work ourselves into believing that we are somehow different, and therefore not subject to the normal human frailties that can defeat more ordinary mortals on ordinary missions. We begin to act as if we were physically and emotionally indestructible.[1]

From Scripture's opening stories of Adam and Eve, and Abraham, Isaac, and Jacob, we learn how humans have been driven by personal hungers—Eve wanted to be like God, and know good and evil; Cain sought

---

1. Hiefetz and Linsky, *Leadership on the Line*, 163–65.

approval for his offerings above his brother's offerings; Jacob sought the blessing and birthright that belonged to his brother, Esau. What, then, are the critical hungers of leaders? In this chapter I have chosen to focus on three of the four issues that have regularly surfaced in our research on case studies of leadership crisis: the hunger for significance, the hunger for intimacy and fear of isolation, and the subtle seductions of greed—the desire for more. Chapter 4 will address the temptation to accrue power.

The "Shadow Mission" of Significance

No leader desires or intentionally seeks to self-destruct. Yet most are vulnerable to self-destruction because of deep, unexamined emotional needs. John, mission leader, and I share a driving passion for success and the accompanying hunger for approval by others of our work. John is candid in his case study, "In my immense pride with being known for my accomplishments, my shadow mission for respect and notoriety took over, and I defaulted toward goal orientation."

As I reflect back over a lifetime, I see how the quest for excellence has become what John Ortberg, in a sermon at the Willow Creek Summit, termed a "shadow mission"[2]—a personal quest to achieve recognition for performance, and a hunger that for leaders like John and me is never satisfied. John cites "immense pride" in accomplishments, and a drive to protect the respect and renown that he has earned from them. For me, in contrast, the hunger seems to run deep in my emotional being. No matter what I accomplish, it is imperfect; and no matter what the recognition, I am not looking at my past honors, but wondering how to get better and what the next honor might be. At this point in my life (retired), I look back and see how foolish these feelings are, and yet I still find them surfacing from time to time.

We have found that many church and mission leaders in our case study data have been driven by similar quests for positive contributions, that when unmasked are in reality the hunger for significance. Most often it surfaces in the desire that people in ministry have to make a difference; women in the research sample often cite this emotional need. Wendy states, "I have literally said to my accountability peer group that I want to contribute to make a positive difference in students' lives." Amy confesses, "I resonate most with the desire to contribute and make a positive difference

2. Ortberg, "Leader's Greatest Fear."

in a complex and constantly changing world, but I also realize the absolute need for courage to effect this."

While "making a difference" has a high value for many women, they also recognize that they work in a world dominated by men, which increases the challenge and the risk. Not only is courage required, but also the understanding of different organizational cultures and the politics of leadership. For some women, becoming significant in a masculine world may mean surrender to the seduction of a role, and losing one's sense of who one is in Christ. Wendy addresses this fear: "I don't want to live or lead out of a seductive need to feel important or make a significant contribution for self-promotion."

Male and female leaders frequently define worthy tasks—writing curriculum, creating programs, serving as ministry consultants, or taking on a challenging ministry program—as their means to significance. As each recounted their ministry crises, inevitably they were not appreciated for their work, and the people they sought to serve rejected, or even worse, ignored them. Joanna discovered that her "desire to bring a new Bible study method became stronger than [her] desire to see these women learn how to study the Word for themselves." Jim found that his hunger for affirmation led him to accept an impossible challenge, and then to work harder in hopes of gaining approval, without success. Once Jim discovered this "secret" about himself, he concluded that managing this hunger is crucial to his success in ministry, and he needs the help of others to break this habit. Others, like Joanna, have realized that they had the wrong priority, and they have sought to refocus ministry away from "offerings" of curricula or programs to investing in people and relationships. All have come to see that their quest for a "positive contribution"—unmasked as a hunger for significance—has become a distortion of their identity in Christ, and the idolatry of self-achievement.

The Fear of Isolation, Intimacy Lost

John, whose story opens the chapter, is what I call an "influence leader," taking great pride recruiting and equipping people to create development projects that contribute with public impact in their community. The crowning moments for him occur when the team functions together as one unit, making meaning both for themselves and the people they serve. However, in his leadership crisis, when the overwhelming demands of the project and his command/control response led two team members to disconnect, John experienced a deep sense of isolation and betrayal. "I have invested so much in these guys; how could they leave me like this?"

Senior pastors often have experienced the same isolating effect. Men and women alike have reported to us that when they have a ministry crisis they often feel utterly alone in their pastoral role, and oftentimes in the normal course of ministry. The dozen or more African American female pastors who have studied with us agree that accepting such a call to ministry before one marries usually destroys any possibility of marriage, and limits the kind of female friendships that one ordinarily has in a church community. Janice speaks for many when she says,

> My greatest "self" issue is not pride or recognition or any such hunger; it is the void of female friendship in ministry—the hunger for intimacy. I can deal with it through awareness, calling on the grace of God, and appreciating the family, friends, and teammates that God has given me. Those relationships are particularly important.

Lezlie Kennedy reports that twenty-three of the thirty African American women seminarians that she interviewed were either single or divorced, with the implication that to become a pastor in this culture was almost certainly a sentence to a life devoid of marital intimacy. These women also reported struggles with doubt (nine), internal conflict (six), low self-esteem, and lack of mentors and affirmation in their ministry.[3]

The greatest danger of our hunger for intimacy lies in the seductions of our needs for emotional and physical connection with others. In a time of significant personal and spiritual crisis, Barry, a missionary leader in an Asian culture, yielded to the temptation of emotional intimacy with a woman other than his wife. While the relationship was not sexual, the consequence for him was the loss of his marriage and his ministry.

Perhaps more challenging is that this hunger for intimacy may also lead us to turn from our spiritual resources and strengths to other impulsive or compulsive responses. When a ministry crisis leads to isolation from others and from God, the behavioral consequences can be self-destructive behaviors, such as extramarital affairs, or addiction to pornography, sexually explicit entertainment, or other forms of self-abuse. For many in ministry, the agony of even a single event of adultery can destroy a lifetime of preparation and effective ministry service.

3. Kennedy, "Call Narrative," 72–77.

The biggest surprise for me when I accepted the invitation to serve as provost and senior vice president at Biola University was the loss of my faculty friends. In my memory, the loss was sudden and painful. I had joined two faculty friends for lunch in the Biola cafeteria the day after the president announced my appointment. The conversation almost immediately turned to my appointment, and as we talked I felt an increasing distance between us. I was no longer Sherwood, colleague and friend; I was Mr. Provost, who had moved to the "dark side" of administration at the university. I was stunned at a change in my emotional relationships with them that I could do nothing about.

The emotional distress of this "void of friendship" affects people differently. As an introvert, my close friendships were always limited, so while I found the isolation of my new role a surprise and at times quite lonely, this was not traumatic for me. My wife was and continued to be my closest friend, and I formed close but occasional friendships with a few missionaries who had been former students or colleagues. When my job became overwhelming, these people were usually there for me, and I found support and comfort in these relationships.

For Janice and others, support from family and friends is crucial. Sometimes teammates may be an important support, yet there are times when they have become part of the crisis, and add to one's personal distress. For many of the women in Kennedy's study, the support they need is just not available to them. For men, disclosing their hunger and seeking relationships of support from ministry partners and family is essential.

The Hunger for More (Greed)

A charismatic apostle who founded a large, very successful church in Southeast Asia perceived leadership authority as a divine appointment and command, "given first in a vision to be a preacher and later on, a prophecy calling him to 'raise a spiritual army for the Lord.'" The founder developed core leaders to serve under his authority and deployed them to start new works. He also started a center for training workers to plant other churches. The founder interpreted the "method of training in terms of a protégé waiting upon the elder so that the anointing will be passed on." The training program also fostered community, with the founders taking the role of spiritual parents to those who followed them. The apostle's home church served as the central headquarters, and the largest of all the family of churches. He retained "divine authority" and oversight over all finances, building efforts, and leadership appointments within the family of churches.[4]

Out of the center for training, the apostle assigned graduate ministry "interns" to plant churches in different parts of the country. After learning the principles of self-governance, self-support, and self-propagation in her training, one female intern reported, "They don't care how you do it as long as the church produced results." Her church plant became very effective, and was self-financing from its inception. In addition, she contributed tithes, other offerings, and financial reports requested by the founders from the beginning. After fourteen years of growth of her church, the "intern" resigned as pastor, citing the unwillingness of the apostle to honor the principles of self-governance, self-support, and self-propagation. At that point, mother-church officials repossessed the bank account, and all other resources of this church plant. After her resignation, the local church split into Chinese and English factions, with the English following the "intern."[5]

Siew Pik Lim documents how this apostle and several other very successful Asian church planters have drifted from their roles as dynamic, mission-focused church leaders to power-seeking, controlling, and even toxic relationships with followers. Lim notes that some leaders preach tithing "so that the house of God would not be in desolation,"[6] yet use the money to acquire personal assets, such as luxury cars, homes, and children's education. When courageous lay leaders (men and women) dared to question these practices, they suffered public humiliation and ejection from their supporting ministry roles.

The hunger for possessions takes many forms for Christian leaders. Temptation begins in very subtle forms of role recognition by followers—the use of title and honorific language (Pastor, Reverend, Doctor, Apostle, President, Chairman, Honorable, etc.); the marking of power distance (deference, submission, humility, acceptance, honor); and the granting of perks and privilege (parsonage, housing allowance, mileage, car, driver, etc.). Each is part of the culture of church and the larger society in which it is situated, and the values of congregation members often shape these forms of distinction for a leader.

After a time, some leaders may conclude that such distinctions and privileges are normal and in fact a right of his or her office. Much depends

4. Lim, "Touch Not the Lord's Annointed," 46–48.

5. Ibid., 90–98.

6. Ibid., 66.

upon that person's personal culture and life history, and his or her internal sense of value and identity. When the leader attaches significant value and identity to such role markers, the loss of any one becomes a threat. If someone inadvertently fails to grant the expected right or privilege, the leader may respond with indignation and perhaps anger. Over time, one may drift from gratitude for God's gracious gifts to grasping for more perks and privilege.

In fact, all of the distortions of hungers discussed in this chapter are a form of discontent with God's provision and purpose. Leaders are tempted to use their authority and influence to acquire the better and best outcomes, more and greater significance, better intimacy, and more perks and privileges of office. The seductions of "office" or "position" are powerful, and for many leaders, personal hunger for more becomes toxic to their leadership and ultimately self-destructive.

The enemies of Christ recount with glee the stories of church leaders who have succumbed to one or another of these self-destructive hungers. The recent history of American evangelical church leaders has multiple stories of the power-seeking, publicity-seeking, sexually unfaithful, and greedy men and women in ministry. The reader can supply names for each category. The saga of self-destruction continues, and as Lim reports, the stories of fallen leaders are repeated around the globe.

Gratitude: The Antidote for Hungers

I remember a critical moment in my early forties when I began to see clearly that these feelings of hunger were undermining my spiritual life; the hunger to be something other than I was denied the wonder and beauty of how God had created me. Further, those hungers diminished the good that God was working daily in my life, and had become a form of rejection of God's blessing and grace. As I wrestled with these feelings, the Holy Spirit led me to an emotional-identity conversion. I began by reflecting back on the history of God's grace in my life—beginning with my decision to quit high school football in my senior year and take typing. That decision was not driven so much by the Spirit, as it was by Walt Rock, a high school classmate playing my same position, who later played in Super Bowl VII as an offensive lineman for the Washington Redskins. In that moment of reflection, I realized that I have been typing since then, and the skill has enabled me to earn a PhD, and to type many manuscripts and books. As I began to count other blessings, the number was so great, I bowed in awe to the God who had created me "in Christ Jesus to do good works" (Eph 2:10).

As I type this manuscript, I thank God for leading me to see God's gifting for my life, and the blessing of following in his pathway. This newfound gratitude, about who I am physically, mentally, socially and spiritually, has brought countless blessings, and increasing contentment about how I perform in the roles that I have been privileged to fill in my life and service.

The challenge for me, and you, the reader, is not to look outward in envy, judgment, and/or condemnation of others, but to look inward. How have our hungers undermined our authority, and increased our vulnerability? John lost his team, and almost lost his project, because of his shadow mission for recognition and success. The apostle lost faithful pastors and undermined his authority and his church-planting ministry because of his hunger for control and money. The challenge of authority and vulnerability is balance; how do we exercise our authority and embrace the challenge of vulnerability when it seems we have lost control? Are we willing to take the meaningful risk to trust God to control what we cannot? Joshua Choonmin Kang and I have found that the discipline of gratitude for God's presence and blessing in the midst of isolation, brokenness, and deficiency restores the balance in our lives and leadership.

In Luke's gospel (12:15), Jesus warns his disciples: "Watch out! Be on your guard against all kinds of greed; life does not consist in an abundance of possessions." In this text, the focus of his warning is broad—inheritance, land, crops, clothing, food, and the general pursuit of wealth. And after the warning, he invites us to consider an opportunity: "Do not be afraid, little flock, for your Father has been pleased to give you the kingdom. Sell your possessions and give to the poor. Provide purses for yourselves that will not wear out, a treasure in heaven that will never fail, where no thief comes near and no moth destroys. For where your treasure is, there your heart will be also" (Luke 12:32–34).

Reflection Questions:

1. In the two cases in this chapter, John and the Asian apostle, what aspects of risk to their leadership triggered their hunger responses?

2. How did each misuse authority and power in their crisis?

3. Which of the three hungers in this chapter—significance, intimacy, more of something (greed)—do you find surfacing in your life and ministry?

4. In your past experience, what kind of risks trigger your hunger response?

4

The Opportunity and Peril of Power

Every kind of ministry role grants some form of authority to the leader, and with authority one also acquires power. The human hunger for power, and the inherent presence of power in all levels of authority, make power-seeking a great temptation for leaders. Given our prior discussion of fear and our tendency to avoid or control any risk that increases our vulnerability, the seduction and misuse of power is worthy of a full chapter of reflection.

I have defined power as having control over some resource, knowledge, relationship, opportunity, or structure that is valued and sought by others.[1] In chapter 1, we learned that Michael and the members of his Reformed church consistory controlled something that was of value to others in their congregation. That control was the basis of their power. Their decision to increase a staff salary from half- to full-time was certainly within their authority, as defined by the denomination and local church polity. As Michael makes so clear, he and his colleagues acted completely within their authority as defined by the rules of their community. Yet the members of that community saw their action as one of the use of power over them, and many responded with resentment and dissatisfaction.

What was the source of their dissatisfaction? The case makes clear that they had expectations for collaboration that were not met. While the authority structure did not require collaboration, the people wanted it, and

1. Lingenfelter, *Leading Cross-Culturally*, 107–8.

perhaps hoped that their pastor would respect them enough to ask. The decision was more important to them than Michael had anticipated, and his exclusion of the congregation became a source of discontent and even conspiracy. The fundamental issue here was consistory control over something of value to them. What was that something? People would probably define it differently; for some it was perhaps conferring a raise without consulting with them, for others it was granting a full-time appointment, for still others it was dissatisfaction with the ministry of the associate, and for all of the dissidents, a decision had been made from power that excluded them.

Control: The Basis of Power in Church and Mission Contexts

Marguerite Shuster defines power as human will engaging some form of authority to achieve an intended goal.[2] This is the perfect definition of what happened in Michael's case; he and the members of the consistory exercised their wills to use their authority within the Reformed church structure to achieve a full-time appointment for an intern. In all ministry structures, mission or church, leaders use their wills to engage the ministry authority available to them for a purpose that they believe and intend for good, but may not be the will of the people. This is the exercise of power in church relationships. When people discern this, as in Michael's case, they may feel that the leaders have "powered" an outcome, and decide to dissent and even disconnect from that community.

As we read Michael's case study, it is hardly a crisis, as we might understand and define that term. No lives were threatened, the viability of the church was not at stake, and it is highly unlikely that any member could possibly have suffered loss from their decision. Yet, for Michael it was a leadership crisis. Why? Because people were not following!

When people are not following, we are not leading. And if we occupy a leadership position, we make the assumption that people will follow. That is a precarious false assumption. There is nothing about a position, title, or role that makes one a leader. Positions, titles, and roles confer authority, as Michael makes clear in this case study, and he used that authority. But people are the ones who make the decision about leadership—they decide if they will follow or not. In Michael's situation, it became very clear to him that many were not following, and they had become critical of his

---

2. Shuster, *Power, Pathology and Paradox*, 94–95.

leadership. In a congregational community that "calls" or elects their minister of word and sacrament, this is a crisis.

Does the Type of Church Structure Make a Difference?

The four case studies presented in the preceding chapters tell the stories of leadership crises in each of the four major types of authority structures for congregational leadership (see figure 4.1): Michael exercised corporate leadership in a Reformed church structure; Timothy exercised consensus leadership in a congregational or covenant fellowship church structure; John exercised influence leadership in an independent, team-focused mission ministry, and the apostle exercised apostolic leadership in an independent, authoritarian Charismatic church. All of the structures confer power on leaders in different ways.

Figure 4.1
Four Types of Congregational Authority Structures

Apostolic Leadership	+ LARGE PDI	Corporate Leadership
Mega-Churches Apostle sets direction Apostolic authority Apostolic property Closed books re: $$		*Denominational Churches* Board sets direction Leader/Board authority Corporate property Policy control re: $$
– INDIVIDUAL		COLLECTIVE +
Independent Churches Personal vision direction Leader shares authority Contract Property Competition for $$	SMALL PDI –	*Covenant Fellowships* Consensus sets direction Elder authority Consensus Property Consensus re: $$
Influence Leadership		**Consensus Leadership**

Underlying these structural types are, following Hofstede,[3] two sets of human values: first, the degree to which people value "large or small power distance" (PDI in figure 4.1) in their relationship with leaders, and second, the degree to which people value "individualism or collectivism" in their congregational relationships. When the perception of power distance is large, people expect leaders to have authority, responsibility and privilege

3. Hofstede et al., *Cultures and Organizations*, 60–61, 90–92.

quite different from the followers, and relationships are defined as between superior and subordinate persons. When the perception of power distance is small, people see leaders as first among relative equals, and relationships are either negotiated or collaborative. The second variable, individual or collective, focuses on whether people expect the leaders and structure to protect and support the interests of the congregation as a whole (collective) or give priority to the interests of the individuals within a congregation. The interaction of these variables generates the four types of structure and leadership:

1. Apostolic—large power distance focused on individual interests;

2. Corporate—large power distance focused on collective interests;

3. Consensus leadership—small power distance focused on collective interests;

4. Influence leadership—small power distance focused on individual interests.

In "influence leadership" ministries, such as John's mission team (also Vineyard and Calvary Chapels), the distance between the leader and follower is small, and they understand biblically that the Holy Spirit confers power in the form of spiritual gifts on all members, and the priesthood of all believers is emphasized. The relationship between leader and members is one where the leader's vision sets direction, while matters of authority, property and finance are negotiated with the input of trusted others.

In "consensus leadership" ministries, such as in Timothy's case study (also Brethren, Church of Christ), people have a similar view of small power distance, but a much greater emphasis on community, consensus, and a covenant relationship among members. Authority is always shared, theoretically equally, among leaders and the consensus community.

In "corporate leadership" ministries, such as Michael's Reformed congregation (also Presbyterian, Baptist), the distance between leader and follower is marked by the clear and distinct role of the minister of word and sacrament. All others have lesser status, but the consistory forms a group of ruling members who have been given authority by and for the congregation. The consistory provides a corporate balance to the authority conferred on a pastor, and the congregation provides a corporate balance to both.

In "apostolic leadership" ministries, such as the Asian apostle (also Episcopal, Methodist denominations), the leader is given special, "untouchable" spiritual authority, far above others in the ministry. The power is held independently of the community, and is often considered a divine appointment. Matters of authority, property, and finance rest solely in the leadership of the apostle and the hierarchy of ministers who have been delegated authority by the apostle.

The point of this brief discussion is that while structures of authority are always present, leadership is about people and leaders who exercise human will to engage any structure for the glory of God or of self. I have argued in another context that "the criteria for good leadership are not formal or structural."[4] Regardless of structure, leaders and followers may and do use their personal will to engage that structure in such a way that they bring crisis or blessing to their congregations. Leaders often exclude and overrule their people, and people often feel intimidated and unable to question a leader. When this happens, people have the power to submit or resist, to follow or to seek an alternative community for spiritual growth and service.

The Temptation to Accrue Power

Once a leader has been granted authority, the temptation to accrue power is inherent to the position and its duties. To have authority usually means that one is responsible to assure that something is done well, or at least to the satisfaction of those who have placed you in that position. A very normal emotional and reasoned response is to accept that challenge, take charge, and assure that the job is done well. However, within this very normal and expected use of authority, there is always a dark side—fear that someone will spoil my work, will thwart my will, or will seek my position.

Jeff, pastor in an American denominational church, after processing his case study of crisis with his peers, describes his discovery:

> I crave control. I am comfortable when I perceive that I am in control of things, and am uncomfortable otherwise. The reason for this is that I truly believe that I know what is best. To maintain the control that permits me to do what I think is best requires that I use power. I have become fairly proficient in understanding and acquiring the various types of power that exist in the organizations I lead.

4. Lingenfelter, "Defining Institutional Realities," 64.

Jeff's experience is actually fairly typical of leaders. Without even thinking about it, he has succumbed to the idea that "I know what is best," and he therefore works hard to manage each situation to achieve that best. To achieve that "best" he has conceded to the deception that "control leads to good," and that exercising power over others will accomplish the goals of his ministry.

But the apostle and many other high-power distance leaders—Asian, African, and Latin—find biblical and cultural grounds to legitimize their command/control leadership. When the apostle knows what the congregation needs or should be doing and thus directs the people this way, the people gladly do it. They, people and leaders, don't see this as craving control, but rather that pastors have been given a sacred authority and responsibility to lead people who need to be led, like a good shepherd. Indeed, in the early years of the apostle's ministry, his church flourished under his controlling leadership. But the dark side of such power is ever present, and the leader who fails to recognize this and submit self to Christ, faces as much or more danger than leaders in other ministry contexts.

Shuster proposes that evil is best understood as "*disruptions of structure and/or will*—the Devil spoiling what God has made."[5] When we use our will to achieve "what is best," rather than take the more difficult path of testing alternative bests in the diverse lights of Scripture, we serve the devil rather than God. While our motivation appears to us to be for good, we accept the false path of "my way," we pervert social and relational structures by judging those who may disagree, and we rigidly cling to our means and ends in the pursuit of that good. The end, then, is of our creation, and the outcome is not God's, because we have not respected and loved God's people, or our enemies.

When leaders are young and inexperienced, they are particularly susceptible to relying upon control to achieve outcomes, often with long-term cost. And when leaders are old (especially in cultures that honor the old), they are susceptible to relying on control because of entitlement that comes with age, and they too do not respect and love God's people and incorporate them in deciding the best.

However, most leaders do not have a conscious awareness of a deeper emotional hunger around issues of power and control. This hunger may be present, but does not rear its dragon-head until one experiences a situation of crisis, a crisis that disrupts the normal routines of work or ministry.

5. Shuster, *Power, Pathology and Paradox*, 140, emphasis original.

When others oppose the leader's will, he/she feels deep emotion, including anger and fear. Given these emotions, the temptation is great to use one's power and control to correct the situation and achieve the sought for goal.

Power Struggles: Direction, Authority, Property, Finance

If we compare the cases of Michael and Timothy (Chinese church planter in chapter 2), it is clear that Timothy had a philosophy of ministry quite different from Michael's. Timothy believed in collaboration, and sought it at every step of his leadership, while Michael believed in corporate structure, and the delegation of authority to the elected consistory. Yet, each faced significant struggles over power issues in their ministries. Through a careful examination of these two cases, we can identify four power issues that are inherent in all ministries: direction, authority, property, and finances.

In Timothy's case, he and his board first struggled about the direction and focus of the ministry. The church began as an English-language ministry for second-generation immigrants and others in the local community, forming a multicultural community of outreach and worship. Timothy's subsequent vision to start a first-generation Chinese-language ministry was not shared by the members of his board or his congregation; but Timothy was persistent, seeking collaboration and consensus before moving forward.

Timothy's second major conflict arose about the acquisition, use, and maintenance of property. Property issues always generate divergent opinions—to lease or to buy, to work together to maintain a land/building gift for future opportunity, or to rent a facility without the burden of maintenance? Timothy preferred the gift option, but board member Thorn wanted nothing to do with maintenance. Getting consensus was impossible, so Timothy framed a compromise to do both.

Timothy's third major conflict surfaced two additional issues: funding and authority over ministry. Thorn, who led ten or more families to leave the church, cited authority and control of ministry as his key issue. While Timothy could dispute this, the underlying issue remains—these two men had different visions for ministry, and in their consensus-based structure, this struggle could not be resolved.

While Michael had a similar conflict about funding and authority in his Reformed church context, the structure was very clear, the consistory had the authority. Yet, both experienced the loss of followers. Therefore, the power issues are not about the right or wrong structure, but rather about the use of power and control as leaders seek to resolve situations of conflict.

For all Christian ministries, the control of money and resources is the most common subject for tension and disagreement. In Michael's case, the decision to increase a pastor's salary from half- to full-time employment provoked significant congregational discontent and the loss of followers. In Timothy's case the decisions to expand facility and staff expenses, even with the formal support of both his board and congregation, provoked the abandonment he feared, with more than ten families leaving his congregation.

The case of the Asian apostle highlights how the use of "divine authority" and unchallenged control may lead to the worst of power abuses, what Lim and others term "toxic" leadership.[6] The leadership crises in this case unfold over a twenty-year period, with many challenges by followers, turning what began as a dynamic, spirit-filled church movement in Asia into a family of churches without vision, focused upon the maintenance of cash flow and the preservation of facilities, income, and the lifestyle of the apostolic founder and his family. While many loyal members continue to support the apostle, the growth of churches has faltered, and many former followers have been forced or have chosen to leave the ministry.

Using Power to Avoid Vulnerability

At this point in the book we have briefly considered five case studies of leadership crisis: Michael, Timothy, John, the apostle, and me. In each case, the leaders have embraced and worked within very different structures of ministry. Each has held a position of authority, and sought to use that position in ways that were consistent with their authority and structure. Yet in each case these leaders made decisions and exercised their leadership in such a way that they lost followers. Therefore, the challenge of leadership is much more complex than position, structure, policy and implementation. It is fundamentally about how and why leaders lead, and how they exercise the authority and power inherent in their position. Working from these five case studies, and from quantitative data gathered in the larger sample of 129 leaders (see table 4.1), let's examine the motivations that leaders report for their use of power.

6. Lim, "Touch Not the Lord's Annointed," 9.

TABLE 4.1 Diversity of the ATS Sample of Leaders			
Ethnicity	Total #	Male	Female
Anglo-American	59	47	12
African American	32	16	16
Latino-American	9	7	2
Korean	8	5	3
Chinese, Vietnamese	11	10	1
Indian	4	4	
African, Haitian	6	6	
Total	**129**	**95**	**34**

John and Timothy are quite open about their drive for success. Their passion surfaces in the details of each case, and it is this deep desire for success that moves them to take command, and to use the power inherent in their roles. Forty of the leaders in our sample (31%) reported this same passion and motivation for the actions they took in their leadership crises.

Michael, in contrast, tells us that his priority was efficiency and effectiveness. He clearly knew the rules of leadership in Reformed church communities, and he believed he was following best practices for the good of the community. He was confident in this fact, and shocked when people did not see the appropriateness of his behavior. This motivation is even more common than the drive for success. In our sample, 101 (78%) report using command and control to achieve what they believe would be the right outcome, and consistent with the values of their people. Michael's case illustrates this well: concern for process, efficiency in the use of time and allocation of resources, and protection of the values of the Reformed community.

Timothy had a very different process, but he also sought the right outcome for all of his people, and gave particular attention to his rival, Thorn, who often opposed his thinking. Timothy lost power to Thorn on each of the three issues in his crisis, and was forced to compromise his agenda and vision. In our sample of leaders, Timothy is not alone; 37 (29%) of these leaders struggled with rivals who contested with them for power. In some cases, these leaders compromised, in others they were forced to withdraw, and in a few cases the rivals mobilized others to force them to resign from their position.

To have one's authority challenged is almost always a crisis for leaders. Both Michael and John report their feelings when their authority was challenged. Michael and 90 (71%) other leaders in the sample sought to defend themselves, their values, and to restore harmony in their communities. Others, triggered by emotions of anger and fear of loss, exercised more power to correct the crisis. John, in his project, confronted his national colleagues seeking to correct their performance that undermined the unity and success of the team and override their objections. In doing this, he further alienated them, until he was willing to repent and ask for their forgiveness. John, however, is not alone—49 (38%) of his colleagues report using their role and power to protect themselves and to correct (sometimes sinful) others who do not meet their expectations. Finally, the fear of shame for some of the African American and Asian leaders in the sample (17, 13%), drove them to use power against rivals or factions, seeking to control opposition and hostile action surfacing in their communities.

Self-will is the Achilles' heel of authority, disconnecting us from Christ, and setting us on a pathway of coercion and control to get what we believe is best for ourselves and those who follow us. In the data we have examined on leadership crises, men and women of God, called to lead God's people, took the authority that God's people gave to them and, for "good purpose," used its power for something they valued more than the people they served.

Self-will is driven by our fear, hungers, pride, and self-righteousness, and our submission to the pressures of our culture and congregations. Trusting in our authority and experience, and as John noted, yielding to our pride and shadow mission for success and respect, we act to achieve what we believe is right through the use of power. The process is so very subtle, small steps of thought and action: the authority has been given to me; I have the responsibility to make this happen; it is "my right" to do this for the good of all; there are always "naysayers" in the crowd, and people who want the power that God has given to me. So then, we take that authority and use it against the very people God has called us to serve, and later wonder why people are no longer following.

The stories of 129 leaders have convinced me that even small acts of reliance on power to command and control can lead us into crises, some of which ignite a fire that burns far beyond our control. If we could gather these leaders, most would testify that their particular situation of crisis caused them emotional pain, spiritual doubt, and a loss of support among the people they have served. For a few the crisis was so severe that they had to resign; for many the crisis undermined their ability to lead for an indefinite period of time; and for all the sense of joy and flourishing in leadership was lost.

Authority and Vulnerability: Jesus in the Place of Power

The Scriptures point us to a better way, the way of Jesus, who never used his authority and power for his own purpose, but rather his highest priority was "not to do my will but to do the will of him who sent me" (John 6:38). For Christian leaders, discerning and obeying God's will is the only path for the effective use of power. Shuster argues that our only course of correction is to put Jesus "in the place of power as a proper source of healing."[7]

What does it mean in practical terms to put Jesus in the place of power? Andy Crouch suggests that the way of Jesus is best understood in what he calls "the paradox of flourishing." Crouch explains this paradox as "the two dimensions of Jesus' life, his vulnerability in dependence and death on the one hand, his authority in his earthly ministry and his heavenly exaltation on the other."[8] Crouch plots this paradox of authority and vulnerability on a two-by-two chart, which I have adapted in figure 4.2 below. Crouch argues that the goal for all human life is flourishing, and for leaders that ideal happens when the interplay of authority and vulnerability is somehow balanced, as illustrated in the paradox of the life and ministry of Jesus Christ (Phil 2:6–8). However, when we fail to balance these two dimensions of our lives and leadership, we end up in one of the other three quadrants—exploiting, suffering, or withdrawal.

Figure 4.2
Authority and Vulnerability in Leadership Crises*

EXPLOITING 71 (55%)	Authority	FLOURISHING
Command/success 40 (31%) Command/control 101 (78%) Override to correct 49 (38%)		
		Vulnerability
Avoid Shame 17 (13%) Avoid Conflict 39 (29%)		Protect Self, Values 91 (71%) Loss of Position 13 (10%)
WITHDRAWAL 37 (29%)		21 (16%) **SUFFERING**

*Adapted from Crouch, *Strong and Weak*, 4

---

7. Shuster, *Power, Pathology, Paradox*, 209.

8. Crouch, *Strong and Weak*, 13.

To reframe Crouch in Shuster's terms, we flourish when we incorporate the wholeness of Jesus—his authority and his suffering—into "the place of power as a proper source of healing and will." But, when we somehow lose touch with the wholeness of who Jesus is and with the power of his Spirit working in us, we then either default to power and exploit those we seek to serve, or default to suffering to be exploited by them, or withdraw completely—overwhelmed by the pressures, opposition and suffering of ministry.

As we have seen in the five stories and the excepts from many other stories of crises reported by 129 Christian leaders, none were flourishing during or after their crisis. After reading Crouch, I examined again all 129 stories to better understand where each had lost their way, and what happened to lead all away from the place of flourishing in Christ. I have presented a summary of that data analysis in figure 4.2. The most obvious insight from my analysis is that the flourishing box is empty—none of the leaders in this research experienced flourishing in the midst of their time of crisis, and many did not experience flourishing until after they had reflected on the how and why of their crisis with others in their doctor of ministry cohort.

The most intriguing pattern that emerges in these stories is that of leaders *vacillating* between exploitation and suffering, exploitation and withdrawal, and suffering and withdrawal. By their own testimony, the crucible of their crises brought many to a place of *suffering*—seeking to protect themselves from wounds, shattered expectations, and thwarted values (91, 71%), and in a few cases the devastation of forced resignation (13, 10%). However, the vast majority of these 129 leaders in crisis fought back, *exploiting* in some way to gain the upper hand in their crisis. Some used their power to assure that they achieved their will and success (40, 31%), in spite of the damage it did to others; most (101, 78%) used command and control as their primary strategy to manage the crisis; and others chose to override the opposition, using their authority to correct what they perceived as error among the people (49, 38%). Finally, a significant number chose the pathway of *withdrawal*—avoiding conflict (39, 29%) or shame (17, 13%), and escaping in ways that protected themselves, but abandoned others to rival leaders or to whatever end the crisis portended.

Crouch argues that suffering, exploiting, and withdrawing all stem from false choices about authority and vulnerability. The data in this research confirms his conclusion: at the *end of their crisis situation* the majority of leaders chose exploiting (71, 55%) as their best option and used this to manage their crisis and continue in ministry; a much smaller sample endured what became chronic pain (21, 16%) and continued suffering in their ministry; while a larger group (37, 29%) ended by withdrawing from that particular ministry within a year or two after the crisis.

In the chapters that follow, we will examine more deeply what it means to put Jesus in the place of power, and to discover pathways for leadership in ministry that enable us to flourish, balancing authority and vulnerability as followers of Jesus Christ.

Reflection Questions:

1. Which of the four types of authority structures (figure 4.1) is closest to your ministry context and style of leadership?

2. In the most recent crisis in your ministry, what do you recall about how you exercised your authority to achieve your desired outcome (figure 4.2)?

3. Can you remember having second thoughts, followed either by suffering or withdrawal during your recent crisis (figure 4.2)?

4. In which of Crouch's quadrants would you locate your leadership today?

Part Two

RECOVERING THE PARADOX— EMBRACING VULNERABILITY

5

Exposing "Termites"
That Undermine Leadership

When Judy and I lived on the islands of Yap in Micronesia, termites hungrily devoured anything constructed of wood or paper in the villages and towns. We had an office in an old bookstore of the Protestant mission, where we worked during the day, and sometimes stayed overnight. In the small side room where we had cots for sleeping, the mission had stored paperbound copies of the Living Bible on a metal bookshelf. One day I pulled one of the many copies off the shelf to read the Scripture. I opened the book only to discover that the inside had been completely consumed by termites. I pulled off a second copy, and it too was a hollow shell. The termites had devoured each of more than twenty copies of these Bibles, leaving them intact on the outside, but hollow and empty on the inside. I examined carefully the metal shelving, and discovered a termite tunnel up the back wall, with a small tunnel bridge across to the first book on the end. From that point, the termites bored a tiny hole in each book, and consumed the interior without any obvious effect on the covers.

The metaphor here is that these books had an appearance of wholeness, of authority, and of strength, but inside they were empty, completely devoid of all of those qualities. The book itself was hollow, easily crushed. The authority of word was completely lost, its substance and content eaten away. And the wholeness was an illusion, sustained by the book spine and cover alone. If we reflect on Crouch's model of flourishing, these books

represent the empty, withdrawal quadrant, the complete absence of authority and of vulnerability. The books were worthless and thrown into the sea.
As we reflect on the crucibles of crises in our leadership, we must ask the
question: how far have the "termites of self" ravaged us in our crisis, and
what can we do to destroy them?

The "termites of self" provide a metaphor for how our hungers, anxieties, judgments, fears, and emotional and physical needs eat away at our
inner being until we are emptied of the word of Christ, depleted in our will
to follow Christ, and no longer able to listen to the Holy Spirit or to worship
and give glory to God. Our external self looks unchanged to the world;
like those Living Bibles on the metal shelf, we seem wholly together to the
public eye. Yet, when we are called upon to lead in crisis, our emptiness
quickly becomes evident to anyone seeking the power and presence of the
Spirit of Christ, and sometimes in desperation, we withdraw.

The Cost of Hiding One's Weakness

The leaders of Israel in Scripture and the leaders of Christian ministry today
share in common their humanity with all of its perplexity and weakness.
And one of those weaknesses is to ignore and even resist signals from God,
and the community, that our leadership has somehow gone astray. The
Chronicles are filled with the stories of one after another leader in Judah
and Israel who, under the pressures of extended family, internal politics,
and external threats, and their own hungers for power, significance, and
security, led the nation in pathways that were ultimately disastrous for all.

The message of Scripture is consistently the same; God pleads with
leaders and people to hear his prophets and apostles, meditate on his word,
and turn from their self-driven ways to obey and serve God. God has cov-
enanted with them to satisfy their hungers for security, significance, and
well-being, if they will only obey the commands he has given them, honor
his name, and commit themselves to his service. Yet in the midst of political
and economic turmoil, God's leaders often doubt his word, seek counsel
from the powerful people closest to them instead of God's prophets and
apostles who challenge them, and take matters into their own hands.

The tragedy is that religious leaders, then and now, are not essentially
better or different from political leaders. Driven by the same insecurities,
hungers and fears, they, too, rely on their power, listen to their close and
powerful friends for counsel, and ignore the words of Scripture and the

prophets who challenge them. The experience of crisis in itself feeds feelings of insecurity and shame. Crisis is never just one experience; often a person experiences a series of losses over a long period of time, and the pathway of power that leads to exploitation compounds this anxiety. The realization that people are no longer following comes as a culmination of these smaller frustrations and disappointments.

As we saw in the data in chapter 4, one of the strongest temptations in a leadership crisis is to blame others, and thus avoid responsibility for one's personal role and contribution to the crisis. Some leaders tend to focus on frustrations and disappointments with the people who fail to meet their expectations, and in their frustration, they react in fear and/or anger to deal with these people and move on. These difficult people may challenge one's role, competence, or effectiveness, with the overall effect of undermining one's self-worth and confidence. Under such pressure, some withdraw completely from leadership, and others hang on, enduring the ongoing agony of suffering and frustration.

The Lord's words through the prophet Malachi (1:10–11) have a chilling effect on all of us: "Oh, that one of you would shut the temple doors, so that you would not light useless fires on my altar! I am not pleased with you," says the LORD Almighty, "and I will accept no offering from your hands." When we lose the power of the Holy Spirit, and the blessing of God for our ministry, the ultimate end is the closing of the church doors, and the shutting down of ministries that once had experienced the power and presence of God. Fortunately, God is patient with us, and faithful to challenge us when we drift astray in our personal relationship with Christ and in our practice of ministry. It is this fact alone that should give us confidence to face our leadership crises, even though the process and the shame and grief of our growing self-awareness may become a cause of anguish and even self-loathing.

The Power of Light

The one thing that termites cannot stand is light! In the darkness of their tunnels, they thrive and consume any structure of wood or paper; but smash their tunnels, and they flee for their lives. They cannot stand the power of light. The same is true of the "termites of self." When we expose them to the light of the word of God, and the refining fire of the Holy Spirit, they wither and die. The Scriptures teach us that the word of God is sharper than a sword, and the presence and power of the Holy Spirit brings light and life.

The prophet Malachi (3:2–3) promised the priests and Levites, the religious leaders of Israel, that the Lord they sought would come, but his coming would be a powerful and purifying presence. "For he will be like a refiner's fire or a launderer's soap." The process will be one of trial by fire, with the Lord himself testifying against those who break faith with God, and do not fear him. But the result of his presence is a restoration of righteousness and the presence and power of God's spirit resting upon them.

The Holy Spirit and the word of God are the keys to forging a flourishing leadership out of our crucibles of crisis. In our frailty in times of crisis we tend to cover our nakedness, our weakness; that is why we default to exploitation, suffering, or withdrawal. We forget that our redemption "by the precious blood of Jesus Christ" (1 Pet 2:13–19) has liberated us from these habits, hungers, and fears. The Spirit is the source of light and life, empowering the word to do its work in us.

As Judy and I have witnessed, facing one's crisis among a small community of peers has been a trial of launderer's soap and refining fire. Thankfully, most of the 129 church and mission leaders who processed their crises with us have experienced the transforming work of the Holy Spirit. When a leader and a small group of fellow servants gather, and invite and submit to the presence and power of the Holy Spirit, God's purifying work will always be done. God alone holds the launderer's soap, God alone can touch the mind, emotions, and spirit with refining fire. And God alone sees deep into the heart of his servants, and testifies against those things that we may so easily cover and hide in our public face and leadership presence.

The Crucible: Exposing the Termites of Self to Light

It is critical for a leader to grasp one fundamental truth—the only person in the crisis that the leader can change is oneself. And that is only possible through the indwelling and power of the Holy Spirit. Blaming others, seeking to remove "difficult persons," changing policy or structure all are surface and superficial issues. The deeper issues lie within us, and our despair is symptomatic of brokenness in the body of Christ.

Usually when a leadership crisis ends badly, the leader spends hours replaying pieces of the crisis in his/her mind. Sometimes that focus is frustration and anger with the other parties:

1. Don't they know that I have the authority to do this?

2. Do these people want to vote on what color to paint the walls and what kind of toilet paper to buy?

3. The elders are elected to lead, but when we do, they seem to resent it.

4. We were well within our rights to make this decision without consulting them. Why are they undermining my leadership?

Many leaders seek justification for how they handled the crisis. This path of reasoning is fruitless, and only leads to deeper frustration and alienation with the others involved.

Every crisis involves many people, and it is easy to focus on their failures to meet your expectations as the leader. If you are the senior leader, the problem is often focused on resistance of followers. If you are leading from somewhere in the middle, then the problem may focus on others who are parallel in the structure: "The elders did not show up to the staff meeting but appointed someone to continue the traditional activity and then tell me they were doing it"; or, you may be unhappy with your boss, your boss may bypass you and make decisions without letting you know; or, you may trust a senior advisor who gives you bad advice, "I submitted to Bill's authority and justified the decision by saying, 'Bill has thirty years of experience.'"

To focus on other people and their problems is to miss why people are no longer following you. To judge and condemn them is even worse, because this violates the direct command of Jesus, "Do not judge, or you too will be judged. . . . With the measure you use, it will be measured to you" (Matt 7:1–2). So, what do we do?

The first and most important step is to name the "termites of self" that undermined you in your crisis. The act of naming serves to bring these issues into the light! As long as they are hidden and unexamined, one has no power or will to change. I cannot even pray about things hidden from me, and I certainly cannot participate with the Holy Spirit to change these habits, deal with the fears and hungers that are seeds for my self-destruction. Once they have been named and exposed to light, I have incredible resources available to me—my trusted peers, the Scriptures, and the discerning and transforming power of the Holy Spirit. In table 5.1, I have named the "termites of self" that played a critical role in my leadership crisis at Biola in 1988. The table sorts them, using the topics for reflection developed in chapters 1–4 to illuminate areas of common risk for leaders.

TABLE 5.1 Naming My "Termites of Self" in 1988		
Distortions	*Topics for Reflection*	*Naming My "Termites of Self"*
Default Habits	"Lesser" ministry goals Value that divides Performance mentality	Resolve the conflict quickly Protect legal interests of the university Get it done! Satisfy the many
Dark Fears	Guilt, shame False assumptions Judging others	What if I look bad on this first crisis? Time was fixed Chair is a "difficult person"
Hungers	Excellence/significance Isolation/intimacy	Messy problem, protect president It is my responsibility, do it alone
Power	Command/control Exploit for good	I had the power, use it Serve "good" of the whole, sacrifice chair

Once we have named the termites, we need the support and accountability of the body of Christ to help us change. In 2008 at the Overseas Ministry Study Center, I invited twenty international church leaders from Africa, Asia, and the Middle East to be a "community of prayerful love" for me,[1] and I shared with them the most difficult crisis of my leadership career. I gave them permission to "ask, seek, and knock" about any aspect of that case, and invited them to bring to light any of the "termites of self" that undermined me in that case of crisis. That was a profound moment of self-discovery, exposing hidden motives and patterns of thinking that had led me down my pathway, avoiding vulnerability and seeking power. And the Holy Spirit did a powerful healing work in me, leading me to the place where I am today, writing this book.

Why Should You Take the Risk?

So why should you take the risk of opening old wounds, and rehashing a leadership crisis that you have effectively put behind you? The testimonies of two pastors and one mission leader, who have disclosed their leadership crises within a fellowship of prayerful loving peers, illustrate the power of allowing God and our fellow servants to probe deeply into who we are and how we lead.

Karen, a pastor to young adults, writes:

1. Willard, *Divine Conspiracy*, 215.

I am able to see my default patterns. I have often operated as a manager because my focus has been on the outcome of the event or accomplishing a goal. When others did not put forth the same degree of engagement towards the goal, my patterns of response were either to push them or to dismiss them completely. My perceived strength in operating in excellence was often just my hunger for significance and affirmation.

Doug, associate pastor, writes:

My case study revealed my greatest fear is rejection and being sidelined so I cannot make significant contributions. I avoid situations where I could possibly fail. My fear of rejection and hunger for approval keeps me from taking risks, I often disqualify myself and hide in circumstances instead of leading.

Dave, mission executive, writes:

In my case review, C asked the question, "What is the hunger that drives you?" . . . I convinced myself that I was a low power person, but those friends have rightly told me that I use power, position, and privilege to get what I want. While I may have achieved some short-term gains with high power leadership, they came at a high cost. . . . As a high-power leader, I felt that I did not need to communicate to others or be accountable for actions and decisions that I had the right to make. I lost out on having the wisdom and help of many counselors.

The testimony of these three illustrate how each person was driven in some way by their need for significance and affirmation; yet each played out their role in a different way. Karen notes that her drive for excellence led her to ride roughshod over people, missing God's mission to make disciples of those she leads. Doug, in contrast, avoided any situation where crisis was a possibility, missing God's invitation to step out in faith. Dave describes how he used his authority and power to achieve what he wanted or thought best for his organization, losing the opportunity to invest in others and draw upon the wisdom of the body of Christ around him. Blindness to self is the common theme among them, and blind people want to see the light of God's presence and work in their lives. The power of reflection on leadership crisis is the opening of a leader's eyes to a better way of serving Jesus Christ and his church.

Reflection Questions:

1. What does the metaphor of "termites of self" mean for your leadership?

2. Can you name some of the termites that have undermined your effectiveness?

3. Look at the brief vignettes of Karen, Doug, and Dave, and then write your own short reflection based upon your responses to these questions.

6

Rediscovering Our Authority in Christ

> Therefore, I urge you, brothers and sisters, in view of God's mercy,
> to offer your bodies as a living sacrifice, holy and pleasing to
> God—this is your true and proper worship. Do not conform to
> the pattern of this world, but be transformed by the renewing of
> your mind. Then you will be able to test and approve what God's
> will is—his good, pleasing, and perfect will. (Rom 12:1–2)

In the last chapter, we have learned that the first step in change is to expose
the "termites of self" to light. That, in and of itself, has a profound impact
upon us. Once the dark side of our strengths and the destructive power of
our hungers are exposed to light, the Spirit of Christ within us moves us to
tears of repentance and gives us the will to embrace the grace of God and
submit in obedience to Christ. Yet at the same time, hungers and habits are
just that, and I have learned the hard way over more than twenty-five years
of senior leadership that if I want to change, I must be very intentional
about what must change, and then commit myself to prayer, a deeper relationship with Christ, and the practice of disciplines to break those habits.

But first, I need to re-attune my mind to Jesus's teaching on authority
and leadership. Lee-Barnwell argues that "both authority and leadership
now exist in a paradoxical relationship in which they may be fully present while at the same time be characterized by servanthood and what is

associated with servanthood and even slavery."[1] In biblical leadership then, true authority and true vulnerability of servanthood coexist. The kind of abuses of power that we have seen in chapter 4 are not biblical leadership, but are contradictory to it. Further she argues that biblical leadership "includes the acceptance of suffering and loss by those who would be "great." The "servant leader" who follows Christ's example depends on God alone, not on a position of influence and power, for identity."

If we are to fully embrace our authority in Christ, we must understand this fundamental paradox; Jesus rejected the kind of authority common to the Jewish, Roman, and contemporary world. "You know that the rulers of the Gentiles lord it over them, and their high officials exercise authority over them. Not so with you. Instead, whoever wants to become great among you must be your servant, and whoever wants to be first must be your slave—just as the Son of Man did not come to be served, but to serve, and to give his life as a ransom for many" (Matt 20:25–28). In the same way, the apostles and writers of Scripture speak of themselves as servants or slaves of the Lord Jesus Christ. In essence, there is no authority in Christ without vulnerability. Our calling in Christ as leaders is to accept the authority given to us by his church and from his word, and to exercise it in the same kind of humility, sacrifice and suffering that he endured for us (Phil 2:1–6).

The Leadership Dilemma of Authority and Vulnerability

A common dilemma of leaders in situations of crises is to wonder, "Where is God? Time is running out!" This false assumption about time is pervasive in the short-term orientation that characterizes American culture and leaders. Under this artificial pressure of time, many leaders take the next step—Joe writes, "I have realized that when I am in crisis or conflict I tend to . . . take a high-power approach to leadership and take back control of things. I will make the decisions for the people instead of making decisions with people." Joe, a church planter in the Eastern United States, makes a common assumption behind taking power, "there is a way (my cultural way), perhaps God is leading me? I can fix it." When we do this, "waiting on the Lord" is forgotten, and we act to "fix it." As Joe notes, discipling and empowering God's people to do God's work is lost, and the only focus is fixing the problem, usually with a technical solution. Joe has failed to

---

1. Lee-Barnwell, *Neither Complementarian*, 174.

see the paradox of authority and vulnerability; he has not understood that to flourish as a leader, he must accept both, and follow Jesus in faith and obedience as shepherd and servant to God's people.

Mary, cross-cultural leader for more than twenty years in Eurasia, has named her personal values as the root of her default habits. Those values and strengths—to be responsible, to trust what you know from experience, to get the job done, to do it alone and on time—are widely shared among Western female and male cross-cultural leaders. As Mary processed her crisis story, the gap between her values and those of her Eurasian church leaders became painfully self-evident. More importantly, she discovered that her pattern of doing things alone and on time disempowered some of her national associates, and inhibited the kind of reflection on their part that she knew was critical for them to meet the challenges of an impending exodus of youth from their faith movement. As she pondered her vision and vocation to these congregations, she concluded that she had to change if she hoped to make a lasting contribution to these local faith communities. To accomplish her mission, she had to accept the vulnerability required to trust others, wait until the Spirit of God moved them to act, and believe that God would accomplish his purpose for these people in a way that challenged her values, tried her patience, and confounded her experience.

For Joe and Mary, reflection on their leadership crisis and default habits has led them to a new self-awareness and understanding of others. Each has gained insight into their personal role in their leadership crisis. But even more importantly, they have learned that there is a dark side of their strengths, values, and practices of leadership. In their attempts to control the situation and thereby reduce or eliminate vulnerability and uncertainty, they have actually undermined the authority given to them in Christ. By usurping the authority of others in the body of Christ, they have disempowered them, provoking passive resistance or open opposition, and undermined the mission of God for his body, the church.

Cooperating with God to Embrace Vulnerability

At this point, it is quite clear that human beings have varying degrees of resistance to vulnerability. For some, anything that might undermine either their honor or their success is dangerous and must be avoided or controlled. For others, some kinds of vulnerability—B or C grades, not getting the best job, serving at tables—are not threatening or diminishing to their identity. But for all of the leaders in our sample of 129, their situations of crisis pushed them into areas of vulnerability where they did not want to go. Further, all struggled in some way with the tension between exploiting and suffering, with the majority giving in to exploitation. Through self-examination in these crises, we all have discovered default habits, or termites of self, that have kept us from embracing the vulnerability of servanthood in Jesus Christ.

Jesus makes it very clear that God alone has the power to prune our lives (John 15:1–5). We cannot cut off the dry leaves and dead wood in our heart, mind, and body. God does this in the power of his Spirit, and it is part of his divine work for those he loves. However, the Scriptures teach us that we may cooperate with or resist God in this process. For example, in Colossians the apostle admonishes us, "Put to death . . . your earthly nature . . . lust, evil desires and greed, . . . rid yourselves of . . . anger, rage, malice, . . . put on the new self, which is being renewed in knowledge in the image of its Creator" (Col 3:5–9). When we align our will with the will of God, God works in the power of his spirit to prune these things from our lives. God refuses to make us slaves; he will not remove old habits when we oppose him, and he grieves when we will to go back to those old ways. Yet God is patient, and full of compassion, because we are adopted children, and the blood of the new covenant was given for the forgiveness of our sins. Our new identity in Christ is secure, yet we may be unfruitful sons and daughters because we resist the pruning work of the father.

Mission leader Dave sums up the essential next step in his growth as a leader. "There are many things that the Holy Spirit is revealing that I can do to cooperate with God. My old default habits have been at work in me for some time. With the help of God and others, I will be actively identifying those habits, because I do not want to continue in them." When we have clearly identified the default habits of our leadership, then we may intentionally cooperate with God and allow him to prune them!

Joe, Dave, Doug, Mary, and Megan are seriously engaged with God, seeking to break their default habits. They have all recognized that the first step in this journey is to abide in Christ; many acknowledge that in their times of crisis, they did not feel God's presence, they were dry branches, withered in their relationship with Christ. Each has committed to renew their spiritual life in Christ.

Joe seeks to deepen his journaling reflections on Scripture, to "press into God and look below the surface of my own life to make sure I'm not reacting or leading out of my defaults. I want to lead from the power of the Holy Spirit."

Doug has committed to "set apart daily times to be in the presence of God, practice a weekly Sabbath and schedule three or four retreats each year to enjoy extended time in God's presence, reflecting on my journey, and listening for his direction."

Dave shares, "My identity is confirmed at the Cross. I am dearly loved and valued by Christ. This truth is tremendously liberating as I am now able to recognize patterns and behaviors in my life where I would seek the approval and validation of others. I exhausted myself by allowing others to set agendas that I would try and fill so that I would feel accepted."

Megan, missionary leader in East Africa, shares similar emotions with Joe, Doug, and Dave, "I fear failure because I hunger for acceptance—that if I don't do well, if I make a mistake or things don't turn out as planned, people will reject me." Her response to this fear, however, is in what Hofstede would term a "feminine" rather than a "masculine" way.[2] In her words, she needs to "rally the herd" of "shoulder" friends and family to help her submit to Jesus and draw strength to resist the temptations of the past, and thereby allow the Holy Spirit to empower her to break these default habits.

In a careful review of the reports of eight of the thirty-four women in our data base,[3] all but one of these eight emphasized the importance of support from an accountability group to achieve change, and six of the eight emphasized the need for deep, covenant relationships for their spiritual and leadership growth. In this small sample of eight women, the four common themes in their cooperation with God are a new paradigm of covenant relationship with God and others, a felt need for a support group that encourages and provides accountability, increased empathy with coworkers and the people they serve, and a commitment to continuing self-reflection with the help of others.

In a much larger sample of men (ninety-five), the most common themes are renewing personal spiritual disciplines, observing a weekly ministry Sabbath, retreat sanctuary with God, and doing periodic reflection

2. Hofstede et al., *Cultures and Organizations*, 139, argue that the large majority of women across cultures place higher value on cooperation and relationships with others than on recognition and achievement in the workplace.

3. These eight gave permission to review and cite their work in this book.

and assessment of default habits and change with a mentor or an account-ability group.

In the testimonies above, each person has committed to engage in the practice of one or more spiritual disciplines that in cooperation with the Spirit of God will enable them to let go of a habit or a hunger that has undermined their ministry and leadership. These are very positive actions to cooperate with the Holy Spirit and the local community of faith in which they participate. Yet, none of them address clearly the issue of how to re-store the paradox of authority and vulnerability in their leadership.

Case Study: Restoring the Paradox of Authority and Vulnerability

Amelia, pastor of a multicultural local church in Australia, has tackled this challenge. After reviewing with peers her case of crisis, she concluded, "My default bad habits were related to prideful expressions of my strengths. I have some useful strengths that I have come to rely on. The problems arise when I lean on my own strengths rather than humbly seeking God's di-rection." As she thought more deeply about this, she discovered that each of her strengths had a dark side. For example, her passion for excellence at times colored her attitude with tinges of arrogance toward others who lacked such passion, and a pattern of action that "my way is right" (see table 6.1). Further, she observed that her ministry practice of encouragement could cover a hunger to be loved, and needed. Amelia notes how each of her strengths has a dark side—the hungers to be right, to be loved, to get it done, and to save others.

TABLE 6.1 The Dark Side of Strengths	
Strength	*Default Habits*
Pursue excellence	Arrogance: my way is right
Encouragement	Striving to be loved, needed
Can-do decisive	Hasty decisions, no participation
Problem solving	Messiah-complex, "save others"

Once she had gained this new self-awareness, understanding that her ministry was often based upon self-strengths, she tackled the challenge of change—how to submit to the Lord and "to 'reprogram' my ways of working." She began with theological reflection—why has God given me these strengths, and for what purposes should I use them? By focusing first on the wonder of God and his creative work, and then on Jesus and the glory of his body, the church, she articulated some specific goals for change, each of which demanded more vulnerability on her part. For example, instead of yielding to the temptation that "my way is right," she was moved to consider the diversity of God's creation and the positive presence of other ways of seeing and doing things. Learning from this, she has intentionally sought to resist "judging" and replace it with respect and appreciation that leads to learning from others. By framing goals for change, she was then able to develop specific strategies for what she terms "body-focused" work as a leader (table 6.2). These strategies include surrender of "my way" to appreciate the ideas and solutions offered by others; emphasizing the community's encouragement of one another, building up the sense of body; developing a team approach to discernment and decision-making; and replacing her solutions with provocative questions to provide room for others to contribute creatively.

TABLE 6.2 Embracing Vulnerability to Build "One Body"	
Vulnerability	*"One body" at work*
Respect of other ways of seeing, doing	Express wonder at God's many possibilities
Resist judging, replace it with learning	Trust, appreciate ideas, solutions of others
Surrender "my way" to team decisions	Collaborate, encourage, build sense of unity
Replace solutions with open questions	People creatively contribute to the mission

Amelia concludes, "My role then, as leader, changes. I am no longer looking to negotiate the minds and manage the preferences of individuals and their special interests. My priority now is to help them be God's People, engaged in expressing Godly purposes. To achieve this, the meeting agenda changes. Relationships become more important than tasks. We listen to people's human stories and make explicit their call into covenant community, submitting to one another out of reverence to Christ (Eph 5:21) and not just being saved by Christ, but being saved for Christ."[4]

Will, Word, and Worship—Pathways to Flourishing

Building upon the brief discussion above, all of these leaders have gained new self-awareness, and moved by the Holy Spirit, they have asked the question—how can I cooperate with God to reframe my leadership in such a way that Jesus is Lord in my life and leadership? More importantly, each has understood that their leadership crisis was in large part self-inflicted. They have clearly made the connection between their values, hungers, and default behaviors and their actions in the leadership crisis. They have also understood that the only person in that crisis that they could possibly change is "me."

Given this new self-awareness, they have exercised their wills, and committed to partner with God, to allow God to prune these areas of their lives. Each has, in one way or another, *willed* to expose a "termite of self" to the light of God's spirit and God's people, and in that light to focus anew on God's word and their personal obedience to Christ (see table 6.3). Each has set forth a practical plan for obedience and accountability to God and to others. And each has humbled self before God in worship, acknowledging that it is only by the power of God that a person can change lifelong habits and emotional responses to crises.

Of the three disciplines—will, word, and worship—each serves a crucial role in this transformation. For some the greatest spiritual challenge is finding the will to do the reflection on a personal crisis, and seek God's light in areas of their lives that they have kept hidden for a long time. For others, such as the Asian apostle, the paradox of authority and vulnerability is a foreign concept, alien to their culture and to their practice of leadership. For these people, the greatest challenge is the discipline of listening to the word of Christ and allowing his words and example transform their culture and habits of leadership.

---

4. Koh-Butler, *Getting Back*, 1–4.

TABLE 6.3 Pathways to Reframing One's Leadership	
Will	To expose "termites of self" to the light of God's word and Spirit; To allow God to prune these habits of life; To embrace the vulnerability of "servanthood"; To reframe leadership as "body work" with God's people.
Word	Discover the paradox of authority and vulnerability in Scripture; Reframe your leadership to focus on the roles of "servant, slave" to Jesus.
Worship	Reflect at the wonder of God's creation, the glory of Jesus, and his body; Remember with gratitude God's blessings, people, gifts, and direction; Petition for wisdom and vulnerability as his servant for his church; Allow the Spirit to work to transform you and those who follow you.

For Amelia, it was worship that turned her to a new direction. When she took time to focus on God, the glory of his creation, the wonder of his love and mercy, and then the glory of Jesus, and the glory of his church; she saw more clearly the self-centered character of her leadership and she was deeply motivated to change. Worship moves us to bow in humility, to acknowledge our self-centeredness, and to open us to the power of word and the healing touch of the Spirit. Worship opens us to change—pruning old habits, and framing new ways of obedience to our creator and Lord. Worship fills us with gratitude, remembering the multitude of ways that God has sought us, forgiven us, turned us to the way of life, and blessed us beyond human measure. Once Amelia had worshipped, she was then able to set forth goals to glorify God, and a practical plan for change in how she might achieve that. Without any direction other than word and the Holy Spirit, she embraced vulnerability, and reframed her work to lead God's people in body-focused ministry.

If there is a danger seeking change, it is to take this work of change back into our own hands, to trust in the techniques of spiritual discipline, or the support group, or the other disciplines of will and word, and to fail to grasp our vulnerability and weakness apart from the Holy Spirit. Our case studies of crises show us how prone we are to reject vulnerability; rather, we are quick to take control, and to trust in our intellect, our giftedness, our instincts, and our power. These are the very habits that have led to our crisis in the beginning, and are the roots of leadership crisis from the beginning of human history.

A Prophet's Story: Time for New Clothes and Worship

Joshua, the priest, and Zerubbabel, the governor of Judea, had a leadership crisis. Given responsibility to lead fifty thousand people—exiles who had returned to Jerusalem from Babylon, they had laid the foundations for the temple of the Lord, and then failed to complete it. While they had begun that work with great excitement and joy, after completing the foundations, they and the people stopped for an indefinite period of time amid circumstances of opposition and crisis. The prophet Haggai, messenger of God, confronted them about their lost passion for God and a preoccupation with their own homes and economic priorities. To prepare these men for this work, God gave Zechariah a vision in which Joshua, the priest, stands before the Lord in his filthy clothes, and the angel of the Lord speaks.

> "Take off his filthy clothes." Then he said to Joshua, "See, I have taken away your sin, and I will put fine garments on you." Once they had put a clean turban on his head and clothed him in the presence of the Lord, the angel spoke again, "This is what the Lord Almighty says, 'If you will walk in obedience to me and keep my requirements, then you will govern my house and my courts, and I will give you a place among those standing here.'" (Zech 3:4–7)

As God renewed his call to Joshua, God spoke again through Zechariah to remind Joshua and Zerubbabel that this time, the work will be "'not by might nor by power, but by my Spirit,' says the Lord Almighty" (4:6). In essence, God reminds them of their past crisis, relying on their own strength to build his house, and then points to the pathway to complete the work. God then confirms their calling: "The Lord again spoke to the prophet: 'Do you not know what these [two olive branches] are?' . . . 'These are the two who are anointed to serve the Lord of all the earth'" (Zech 4:13–14). These two men had no less of a role than to serve the Lord of all the earth, for God's mission and God's purpose for his people.

We, like Joshua, in our leadership crises have accumulated "dirty clothes," contaminated by default habits, hungers and even sin. Although we have been completely cleansed by the blood of Christ, we sometimes need a change of clothes. The Scriptures remind us as God's chosen, who are holy dearly loved, to "clothe yourselves with compassion, kindness, humility, gentleness and patience . . . and over all these virtues put on love, which binds them altogether in perfect unity" (Col 3:12–14). The daily discipline of dressing ourselves mentally with these virtues serves as an act of obedience, enabling us to let go of old habits, and to trust God when everything seems to go wrong. It is in our weakness that God manifests his power and glory. In the end, it is God who deserves our worship and gratitude for the joy we discover in obedience, and the wonder of the fruit that God produces through that obedience.

Reflection Questions:

1. How would you articulate the leadership dilemma of authority and vulnerability in your story of crisis?

2. What in Amelia's story gives you insight into how you might process your own story of the paradox of authority and vulnerability?

3. Take a few minutes and think through what Will, Word, and Worship might mean for your leadership future.

7

Embracing Vulnerability to Flourish

Pastors and leaders of Christian ministries experience many challenges in their daily work and lives. Most of these challenges have a routine character about them; they have happened in the past, they will occur again in the future, and we often develop regular processes and even policies to deal with them. My leadership mentor, Clyde Cook, told me that we create policies so we do not have to make the same decision every day. Through the use of policies and processes, we structure systems in Christian organizations so as to make management predictable and somewhat routine.

We typically envision good leadership as something that is vision driven, growth oriented, and effective at managing the unpredictable people and events that could create chaos. Leaders often attend seminars to learn particular tools, such as management by objectives, or the "four frames of leadership,"[1] that will make them more effective. Strategic planning is one of the tools that leaders typically use to articulate an institutional vision, and to frame a leadership agenda that will accomplish their institutional and leadership goals. All of these strategies seek to exercise authority to reduce or eliminate vulnerability.

When I accepted the role of provost at Fuller in 2001, my first responsibility was to lead the institution in the development of a new strategic plan. Working with the administrative team and faculty we accomplished this through a two-year process, developing a plan that we then implemented

1. Bolman and Deal, *Managing Complex*, 1–10.

over a period of five years. Through careful leadership and management, we accomplished more than 75 percent of that plan. When Fuller experienced a financial crisis in January 2009, the trustees gave us four months to restructure the institution. This time frame was clearly inadequate for strategic planning and required a fundamentally different response from me and from the Fuller community.

Adaptive Challenge: High Vulnerability

An adaptive challenge is always about a core issue for change that threatens an organizational community, and for which people tend to either assign blame or avoid responsibility.[2] Heifetz notes that resistance to change is fundamentally grounded in a gap between the values people hold and some aspect of the reality they are facing. As their leader, you have a responsibility to them to define that reality and to lead them to more meaningful and effective ministry or service; yet because of the value gap, their resistance is high, and for leaders, the risk of crisis and failure is high.

The critical indicator of whether a challenge is technical or adaptive is the presence or absence of value conflict. For example, restructuring any organization or ministry is certain to surface value conflicts (see table 7.1). Many people prefer the status quo, and fear that change will undermine something or someone they value. Or, turning routine work, such as weekly worship rehearsals, into a deeper commitment to become followers of Jesus cannot be imposed. People are volunteers, and have values about time and other priorities, and when forced will resist such change. The Lord Jesus invited and challenged people to follow him, and he released those who had other value priorities. When leaders draw from their technical tool kit to address adaptive challenges, the outcome is almost certain crisis, and sometimes the demise of the leader or the people engaged in the controversy.

2. Heifetz, *Leadership without Easy Answers*, 250–76.

TABLE 7.1 Comparison of Technical vs. Adaptive Challenges	
Technical Challenges	*Adaptive Challenges*
Strategic planning	Restructuring staff/lay team for expanding ministry
Rehearsing worship music	Discipling a worship team to work as one body
Teaching series on conflict	Managing factional conflicts in congregations
Sermon series	Discipling "consumers" to be "followers" on mission

All the tools of management are ineffective for such challenges; a time of value conflict and crisis is a time for leadership, engaging people in such ways as to motivate them to be willing and ready to follow. Applying known institutional solutions to address such challenges is futile; policy, process, planning, teaching, and preaching solutions are only effective in contexts and circumstances that are relatively protected from significant value conflicts among the people engaged or from external forces that provoke unanticipated change.

Why are values so important? What role do they play in conflict? The Fuller financial crisis of 2009 was clearly an adaptive challenge. The historic structure of seminary finances divided the community into academic and support divisions. The people serving in both interpreted these divisions as an implicit hierarchy of value; many faculty expressed a higher priority for academic interests and they demanded cuts in the support costs of the seminary. Managers and staff complained that faculty did not understand their workload, nor the need to increase enrollment to cover costs. To make matters even more complicated, the values and priorities of the trustees who mandated the restructuring were often in direct conflict with those of faculty and managers. Trustees imagined that we could move quickly to online forms of instruction, providing a Fuller master of divinity program at lower cost for a much broader constituency. Further, many believed that by using models from industry, we could restructure our internal processes to achieve greater efficiency with fewer people. These very significant value differences were daunting, pushing me and my advisors to prayerfully seek God's wisdom and understand how we might work effectively with the personalities and factions that had become divisive parties in the crisis.

To address an adaptive challenge, it is crucial to understand the value differences embedded in the emotional life and behaviors of the people involved. In order to gain such understanding, a leader must engage in careful listening and observation (prayer, discernment within the body) to identify those issues that threaten the organizational community. Further, the pathway for change will require adaptive work on the part of both leaders and people.

Adaptive Leadership and Adaptive Work

I have defined leadership as "inspiring people who come from two or more cultural traditions to participate with you (leader or leadership team) in building a community of trust, and then to follow you and be empowered by you to achieve a compelling vision of faith."[3] Embedded in this definition is Paul's exhortation in Ephesians that in Christ we are members of one body, and that we work together in unity as part of the body of Christ. Leading, then, is about mutual trust and honor, and about equipping and empowering the people who make up the body of Christ to do the work of ministry.

I will define "adaptive leadership" as leadership that exercises one's authority in such a vulnerable way that the leader is able to inspire and mobilize God's people in situations of crisis to move beyond their personal values and habitual practices toward a greater vision and engagement for the mission of God in that changing context. Such situations demand responses by leaders of a significant difference in kind, what Ronald Heifetz has termed "'adaptive work' . . . work that involves learning required to address conflicts in the values people hold, or to diminish the gap between the values people stand for and the reality they face."[4]

For example, a leader who desires to refocus his congregation to a "missional church" perspective faces significant value challenges. The reality of most churches is that attenders have a consumer mentality, created by the larger culture. To design a sermon series or a curriculum to achieve such a shift in focus is insufficient; this approach assumes that a technical solution with new content will produce significant value change. The work to achieve such a shift in congregational values and engagement is far more

---

3. Lingenfelter, *Leading Cross-Culturally*, 17–18.
4. Heifetz, *Leadership without Easy Answers*, 22.

challenging than a sermon series, and requires significant learning on the part of both leaders and followers.

Heifetz and Linsky suggest two strategies for such learning: first to "get on the balcony" to observe who are engaged and what they are doing, and second to "listen to the song beneath the words" to better understand what they are thinking.[5] To "get on the balcony" is to find a place of perspective where one can see "the dance floor"—a place to observe what people are doing and how they are connecting to one another. As an extension of his metaphor of "the balcony," Heifetz suggests that human actors are complex beings, who rarely disclose all that they are thinking or feeling on a given topic. Therefore, leaders must engage in more careful listening that looks beneath the surface of a story, a discourse on a topic, or explanation of an event. Both of these activities require an attitude of vulnerability that Crouch terms "warmth"; listening to people with genuine empathy and respect, followed by action that demonstrates clearly that one has heard and learned from this process.[6]

In the Fuller financial crisis of 2009, I found it virtually impossible to "get on the balcony" and observe. However, I understood the critical importance of learning what was happening "on the dance floor," so I created some personal windows from which to observe, listen, and learn. Perhaps the most valuable window was a small group of two administrators and three faculty members who became my advisors and decision partners early in the process. I chose to invite them because they were not my supporters (only one reported directly to me), they were actively engaged in some part of the Fuller "dance floor," and I hoped they would objectively observe and listen to those around them.

My invitation to these five was bluntly honest and open:

> I am two years away from retirement, and I want to finish well. The trustees and the president have charged me to lead this process and to present to them a proposal to restructure the seminary in such a way to balance the budget and position Fuller for several difficult years ahead. My role as provost isolates me from the community, and I need to learn what people are thinking and valuing in your part of the seminary. Most important, I need your counsel and correction. I am asking you to give me the advice and counsel that, if I follow it, will keep me from doing something stupid in this process.

5. Heifetz and Linsky, *Leadership on the Line*, 64–67.
6. Crouch, *Strong and Weak*, 7.

I found each avenue of listening and observing important to my leadership learning in this crisis. My decision partners guided me in framing the total process, and their advice was often counterintuitive to me, correcting my misperceptions of how best to involve faculty and others in this strategic work. By inviting these individuals and others to give me feedback throughout the process, I understood better the emotions of the wider community, and discovered and corrected missed opportunities to build trust in my communication with the whole community. It was the act of accepting their correction that gave me credibility in this process.

Once a leader has done the learning essential to understand the value conflicts that drive the crisis, Heifetz and Linsky argue that the next step is to "give back" to the people the challenge of addressing the "gap between values they hold and the reality they face."[7] They wisely counsel that adaptive leadership is most effective when the issue of conflict is so ripe that people are in crisis and willing to do the hard work of change. However, in many situations people are reluctant and even unwilling to consider this work.

To give the work to the people is the ultimate risk, an act of vulnerability, that many leaders are unwilling to take. Further, to do so requires additional learning and using one's authority, or firmness, in a different type of leadership. The role of a leader shifts from command/control for results to using one's authority and power to create a process and a time framework for work, to stay engaged with the people in that process so as to manage conflict and sustain trust, and to keep the people working toward a clearly defined but open-ended outcome. Heifetz and Linsky describe this use of authority as creating a "holding environment,"[8] and they outline four specific applications of one's authority and power to achieve this objective: first, control the temperature and pace the work, second, keep people's attention focused on the issues, third, stay engaged, observing, asking questions, interpreting alternatives, and finally, clarify the scope of work and the decision process toward a defined outcome.

The Use of Authority and Power in Adaptive Leadership

As we have seen in chapter 4, the use of power in leadership is a profoundly complex question, and history suggests that leaders often do not use it well.

7. Heifetz and Linsky, *Leadership on the Line*, 127–28.
8. Ibid., 102–22.

In hierarchical church and mission contexts—Anglican, Methodist, and some Pentecostal denominations—a leader is expected to use the authority and power associated with that role to accomplish the mission of the organization. Some of these hierarchies confer independent power upon the top leaders, while others emphasize shared power between a board and those in leadership roles. In more congregational and collectivist church and mission contexts—Baptist, Brethren, and Church of Christ—the group keeps collective authority over mission and decisions, but may delegate to elders or elected officers the authority to oversee the routine functions of the organization, working in accord with policy. Corporate organizations—Presbyterian or Christian Missionary Alliance—operate within a balanced tension between corporate policy framed by members and delegated authority to one or more executive leaders.

The ways then that a leader might use power for adaptive leadership will vary in terms of the structure of authority and decision-making within the organization. When one has "given the work back to the people," that means different things in different congregational settings. What does giving the work to the people look like in different structures? And what parts does a leader's personality and personal leadership style play in this process? We turn to these questions in the concluding sections of the chapter.

Case Study: A Uniting Church Adaptive Challenge

Amelia, senior pastor and denominational leader in the Uniting Church in Australia, was asked to chair a task force of the Uniting Church to respond to the internal struggle about the possibility of same-gender marriage becoming legal in Australia. She states, "I knew this particular issue could lead to anxiety and conflict within our group, but also noted if we could find ways of working together constructively, there may be some hope for others who are also struggling."[9] Understanding that this was an adaptive challenge, and taking from Heifetz the thought that her power as a leader might be best used to give the work back to the people, she became intentional about "attending to the environment for work, putting in place opportunities in the agenda to raise or lower the temperature."

> From the outset, I explained to the group that we would be working in what would sometimes feel like an uncomfortable space, but

---

9. Koh-Butler, *Getting Back*, 5.

reassured them that I believed we had built enough trust to be able to work at that level for a sustained period. I did give them clear time frames about when we would be doing this work and when we would be taking breaks. I also asked people to be mindful and caring of one another, reminding them that as they all had excellent pastoral skills, I would rely on members of the group to attend to each other's safety and support. I also asked a trusted observer-guest to act as Chaplain should anyone need it.[10]

Amelia is a very relational leader, and understood that in her Australian context, she would be far more effective with the task force by employing relational, rather than command/control strategies. She understood that all on the task force had other work, and that this challenge would deplete their energy and stretch their capacities for effectiveness. She therefore built into their relationships time off from the task, and ways to deal with tensions that inevitably arise in such a process. She understood that as a leader, it was not her responsibility to draft the outcome of the task force; she had given that work to them. Rather she listened carefully to the participants, seeking ways to keep them working together, and collaborated with them to adjust the process and time frame of the work so that they could be most effective.

Contrasting Two Styles of Adaptive Leadership

The Fuller and the Uniting Church case studies offer two very different pictures of how a leader might implement the principles of adaptive work, drawn from Heifetz, Grashow, and Linsky.[11] Using these principles, I have compared and contrasted how Amelia and I used our authority and vulnerability to raise the temperature of our respective constituencies to keep them working. In my case, I am working with employees, while Amelia is working with volunteers who are members of these church congregations. That difference alone forces each of us to think differently about the participants in the process. Yet we both employ Heifetz's principles to exercise authority and vulnerability for adaptive work. Amelia is very pastoral and personal, employing stories, seeking reconciliation in relationships, and encouraging working members to voice taboos, and worst-case scenarios from different interest groups. My leadership is very institutional, employ-

10. Ibid., 6.

11. Heifetz et al., *Practice of Adaptive Leadership*, 133–60.

ing memos, defining tasks, and surfacing power struggles and protected interests (see table 7.2). We share a common goal of keeping people motivated to address and respond to an adaptive challenge for our communities.

TABLE 7.2 Implementing Adaptive Work: Two Alternative Processes		
Adaptive Work	*Fuller Case*	*Uniting Church Case*
Pose tough questions	Memos re: restructuring	Stories of ethical dilemmas
Give people responsibility beyond their comfort	Leadership role—empower to reinvent structures	Pastoral role—empower for reconciliation across church
Surface conflicts	Who has power? Will you implement our decisions?	Worst scenarios, taboos, stories of pain/betrayal
Protect the weak, marginal	Protect faculty, but not VPs, managers, service units	Share weird stories, affirm marginalized and wounded

The nature of the issues in each case had life and death implications. For some employees at Fuller this process would mean loss of jobs, and perhaps close friends. The responsibility for many on Fuller's task forces was overwhelming. As provost, I acted to lift some of that burden by taking responsibility for the actual selection of persons who might be terminated in the process. Thus, a task force could propose the reduction of a vice president, but they could not decide which one that would be. That decision remained the responsibility of the president and provost. For the volunteers from the Uniting Church, whatever decisions they made could have momentous implications for their local congregations and friends. Given the very diverse perspectives on same-gender marriage across the church and within congregations, this assignment was very daunting. Amelia helped the group articulate the limitations of their work and what they might produce from it.

Amelia and I used very different strategies to engage with people to clarify both the scope and decision process of the work. My team emphasis could be described as analytical and structural in nature, encouraging and enabling people to examine data and do hard technical work. We defined issues in concise analytical terms. Amelia, in contrast, led people to examine details of biblical, theological, social, congregational, and community life, expanding significantly their comprehension of related issues. By creating a "thick description of related issues," she challenged her groups to do much more careful reflection beyond the stories where they began.

We both created two task groups, and divided the work between them, but with employees Fuller could demand a much more rigorous time schedule, and also a clear end of the task. The Uniting Church volunteers agreed to work periodically over a six-months period with clear time-specific goals. Thus, we had very different strategies to moderate the temperature to keep people engaged, and to pace the work toward a final outcome.

Avoiding the work is a very common response to such difficult challenges. The role of supporting ligaments (Eph 4:16) in body work is to keep the parts working together in unity. We each chose practical ways to lift the burden of the work and to keep people engaged to complete it. Amelia broke the intensity of their periodic work sessions with breaks for food, worship, fellowship, and storytelling. She also agreed to a time frame with members that set clear goals, but reduced the pressure for resolution. At Fuller, we suspended all meetings to create open time for task subgroup sessions with employees. At the same time, we encouraged teams to focus on achievable goals, and recommend tough issues for longer-term analysis. Weekly reporting from the chairs of subcommittees and each task force insured that the work would continue.

In these two cases, Amelia and I both understood that as leader, it was not our responsibility to draft the outcome work of the task forces. Rather we each listened carefully to the participants, seeking ways to keep them working together, and collaborating with them to adjust the process and time frame of the work so that they could be most effective. And we both stayed engaged as their leader. The nature of this engagement was not directive toward a solution, but rather to define and explain the scope and limitations of their work, and to acknowledge again our responsibilities as either provost or chair to lead them to a substantive response on the adaptive challenges before us.

Managing the Conflict

Conflict is endemic to adaptive work. From the very beginning, the value differences in each community created tension. In my first meeting with middle managers at Fuller, I wounded many with my comment that our existing systems were a cancer that eroded our capacity to adapt to a rapidly changing world. This remark was taken personally by several managers, and created opposition to the process from the beginning. A much wiser Amelia reports:

> I led the way by explaining some of the conflicting issues the dis-cussion raised for my family and my ministry context. I confessed my concern that as the minister of a congregation that welcomed same-gender couples, I might be blinded to the concerns of some members of the group and hoped that this would not compromise my capacity to speak as their chairperson. I recommitted myself to listening attentively and asked the group to help me be fair in my public representations and advocacy related to their concerns.

To manage any conflict requires much humility and patience, again virtues that are part of our calling in Ephesians 4:1–4. In humility, we must listen to the concerns and hurts of other, and respond with compassion. For my part that included a public letter of apology to managers for my cancer remark:

> I was wrong to use it, especially since many interpreted that state-ment as a condemnation of their persons and work. . . . I wish I had commented about the importance and value of each of the diverse persons in the room, and of our call to be the "body of Christ" in this challenging and difficult work. The God we serve values all of the people at Fuller, and his command is that we love, and thus respect, one another.

My most serious challenge came from a subcommittee of a task force. They asked, "How much freedom do we really have, and what confidence can you give us that our work will be taken seriously?" My response to the questions had the potential to unravel a whole month of task force work. I needed to answer in person with both humility and integrity, but also to put my response in writing so that it could not be misinterpreted or distorted. I assured them that they were completely free to make any recommendation with reference to "functions, systems and positions, but not on people or performance." And I also assured them that if for any reason I disagreed with them, I would come and discuss that issue with them face to face. But I also stated clearly that at the end of the process, "after dialogue with faculty, leadership and trustees, I will make my decisions and take responsibility for them."

Embracing Vulnerability and Authority—God's Work

During the financial crisis experienced at Fuller in 2009, the most frequent question asked of me was, "Does this work mean anything, or are you just trying to get us to buy into decisions you have already made?" If it was the latter, to gain compliance and support, no one was interested or willing to work. The point is that when we ask people to do the work, we must respect their findings, and through dialogue with them make sure that their contributions clearly shape the final outcome. By being faithful to our charge as servants of Jesus Christ, we embrace our vulnerability as servants, and we work to build trust and motivation for his people to be the church and to accomplish its mission. And if necessary, we must risk going to the cross, should many of the people demand it.

For Amelia and her Australian colleagues, the value conflicts about same-gender marriage were threatening to the core beliefs and identity of the participants. Whatever the end product of the work of this task force, some in the denomination and on the task force were dissatisfied; further, Amelia may also find that the outcome of the process does not fully represent her values and beliefs. The challenge for these men and women is to trust this work to God, and to keep on praying for the guidance of the Holy Spirit in the places where compromise seems impossible, or wrongheaded. Their commitment to one another in Christ on this question is the only way they can possibly find unity as a body on this issue. The gulf between them as they struggle to integrate Scripture, reason, church history, and experience on this issue challenges the bravest among them.

For both Amelia and me, it was essential to resist taking control, or seeking a particular outcome. To do so would be to undermine the work of the Holy Spirit and the work of the people given the responsibility. At the same time, we must stay engaged, and trust God for the outcome. We, in our different ways, worked to keep the heat on, manage conflict, and confront work-avoidance behaviors. The tensions for a leader in such circumstances are great, so great that Heifetz terms this process as leading "on the razor's edge."[12] To lead on the edge is to risk a fall from power and even death. Heifetz notes that Martin Luther King Jr. died for his leadership "on the edge" in the civil rights movement in the United States.[13]

---

12. Heifetz, *Leadership without Easy Answers*, 125.

13. Ibid., 248.

For both Amelia and me, the most critical understanding of adaptive leadership is that the outcome belongs to God. To flourish as persons in leadership we must embrace both the authority given to us in Christ to serve, and the vulnerability of trusting his people and his Spirit to accomplish whatever God intends. To give the work to the people, and then overrule their decision, leads to distrust, resistance, and even rebellion against the leader and God. The outrage that follows overruling the work of the people is worse than their outrage at one's command/control decision in the first place. And perhaps more importantly, it violates our covenant relationship with God, which requires that we work in such a way as to build up the body so that each part is doing his work toward the end of giving glory and honor to him.

The comfort and confidence we may have in these circumstances comes through our relationship to Christ. As Crouch suggests, in Christ authority and vulnerability come together.[14] We know that the battle is the Lord's, and we are "servants" called by the "master" to do his bidding in this work. We work under the authority of Christ. The churches belong to Jesus, and not to us; the power belongs to God and to God alone. Therefore, we need to renew our covenant with God, not to accrue power for our ends, but rather to empower his people to do God's work. Our task is to obey him, to love his people, and to trust God to accomplish God's purpose.

We are reminded again that God's work is always "body work," and our responsibility is to build up the body and to keep the body at work. In ourselves, we are incomplete, and as leaders we have no authority apart from Jesus Christ. With the authority he gives us, we are responsible to equip the members of the body for his service, and mobilize them to do his work. As we have learned in this chapter, part of that mobilization is to orchestrate the work of the body in such a way that it can sustain, in its diverse and sometimes conflicted members, a sense of unity and purpose, and be accountable for working as one to achieve God's purpose,

> until we all reach unity in the faith and in the knowledge of the Son of God and become mature, attaining to the whole measure of the fullness of Christ. (Eph 4:13)

---

14. Crouch, *Strong and Weak*, 131–32.

Reflection Questions:

1. As you reflect on your ministry, do you see a particular crisis that you would now define as an adaptive challenge?

2. What are some of the value conflicts that seem obvious to you now about that challenge?

3. What does "adaptive work" mean to you, after reading this chapter?

4. What will you "take away" about the interplay of authority and vulnerability, after reading the Fuller and Uniting Church case studies of adaptive work?

Part Three

BUILDING A CHRIST-CENTERED CULTURE OF FLOURISHING

8

Getting the Right Focus: The Glory of God

Lee Ellis, leadership coach and survivor of more than five years as a prisoner of war in Vietnam, makes the profound observation that the most important factor in leading people is to intentionally build and communicate a culture that makes very clear to everyone involved the critical components that you share together, and the way in which that culture reinforces the mission and purposes that unite you. Ellis discovered this principle in his survival experiences as a POW in Vietnam, and has found it particularly applicable for coaching leaders in government and business.[1] As I have listened to the stories of Christian leaders in crisis, I am convinced that is also crucial for effective Christian ministry. However, I do not believe that leaders of church and mission communities can impose a culture upon their people, as some in our case studies of crisis have tried to do. Rather, cultures of ministry must be grounded in Scripture, and formed out of the faith journeys of the participants called by God to participate in that ministry community. These cultures of ministry must be diverse, as the body of Christ is diverse, but at the same time they share at their core biblical truths that are nonnegotiable.

This and the following chapters will suggest and explore what I believe are critical and essential biblical components for cultures of ministry, and at the same time, offer insights as to how these components may be expressed within the diversity of the body of Christ. I am calling these components

---

1. See Ellis, *Leading with Honor*, Kindle loc. 2269–99.

spiritual "pillars" for a house in which God dwells, following the biblical metaphors in the epistles of Peter and Paul. As I have argued in chapter 4, I do not believe that God mandates a particular structure for cultures of ministry, nor specific forms for work and relationships. To the contrary, I find Scripture teaching that all cultures are both "prisons of disobedience" (Rom 11:32) and contexts essential for the communication of the gospel and the formation and work of his body, the church (1 Cor 9:19–23). Therefore, the purpose of these chapters is to explore ways in which the message of the gospel and the power of Jesus Christ transforms people and cultures so that the members of his body and its leaders will flourish as a spiritual house, "a dwelling in which God lives by his Spirit" (Eph 2:16).

Beginning with the End in Focus

When I was writing a book with Paul R. Gupta, I learned what has become for me the most important principle for Christian leadership—to always lead with a clear understanding of the end: what is God's purpose for us on any given issue?[2] This for me must be the corner post, the pillar in our spiritual house, that cannot, must not be omitted.

We are the body of Christ, and God's will for us is to become mature, "attaining to the whole measure of the fullness of Christ" (Eph 4:11–13). The notion of reframing our leadership around God's purpose is crucial to the achievement of this goal for his church. When we start with the wrong goal, we will inevitably achieve what we have targeted in our planning. So why would any leader start with the wrong goal? As we discussed earlier, our cultural values, the pressure of the people we serve, and the habits learned from other leaders in ministry are ever present, and the moment we lose concentration, we drift along, conforming to the habits and practices of our culture.

In his letter to Christians scattered in the Roman empire, Peter understood the cultural pressure on these believers to revert to their old ways and to the cultural pressures around them. So, he reminds them of their incredible new identity in Christ—"a chosen people, a royal priesthood, a holy nation, God's special possession that you may declare the praises of him who called you out of darkness into his wonderful light" (1 Pet 2:9). These words are treasures for the Christian leader, making fundamentally clear who we are and what we should be about.

2. Gupta and Lingenfelter, *Breaking Tradition*, 105–8.

Yet Peter understood the difficulty they and we face in our lives, surrounded as we are by a world of unbelief and living with our own brokenness, hungers, and desires. The phrase "sinful desires, which wage war against your souls" (1 Pet 2:11) is precisely the pressure we face in our ministries. We have every intention of working for the glory of God, and we work hard to fulfill God's purposes in our lives. Yet, we are constantly at war, our own desires undermining us, and the culture around us provoking and affirming our decisions to settle for lesser goals and goods.

I know that Scripture and a daily intimate walk with God are essential to keeping focus. Yet, I have found that in spite of my commitments to sustain these practices, I am blind to my own habits and default behaviors. I read Scripture and am convinced I am on the right path, yet a year or two down the road I look back, having gained deeper self-understanding and discernment, and I grieve at my blindness and settling for lesser goals. As I look back on my own life and leadership, I have found that reflection on my past crises provides many of the insights I need to prepare for the next challenge. I will tell you a story to illustrate this point.

Learning to Refocus: A Ministry Case Study

In 1996, as senior vice president at Biola University, and a member of the board of the Grace Brethren International Mission,[3] I was moved in spirit (or my own desire, I cannot be sure) to lead a student ministry team to Chad. Several leaders in our Brethren churches in Chad had a passion for evangelism, and during a short visit there in 1995, I became aware of the large numbers of unreached people in Chad. I pondered how we as a mission might support these local pastors in their efforts to reach beyond their regions to more than 120 unreached language groups. I learned that these men were limited to travel on foot, by bicycle, or catching rides on occasional trucks of missionaries. I was also influenced by my Biola colleague Tom Steffen to believe that chronological Bible storytelling was a more effective way of communicating the gospel to unreached people.

Being a senior leader at Biola, and committed to mission, I decided to challenge Biola students to consider a short-term ministry trip to Chad, targeting an unreached area, using chronological storytelling and drama to share the gospel with these unreached people. I hoped to recruit men to consider career missions, and so I planned a ministry that would appeal to

3. The mission changed its name to Encompass World Partners in 2010.

these young men, using bicycles for transportation from village to village for this ministry. Working with my missionary colleague Dr. Tom Stallter, we agreed to work with local pastors, and focused on five villages in the south of Chad for this outreach.

The details of the ministry are complex and I will only summarize what happened. Following my convocation challenge at Biola in January 1996, more than forty-five young men and women gathered to hear more. I invited them to join me in a weekly prayer vigil for Chad, and periodic early morning prayer, while riding bicycles along a concrete storm drainage pathway to the ocean. By November of that year six men and two women had persisted, and we began our drama rehearsals for the January ministry. We arrived in Chad in January of 1997, made our way to the city of Moundou, and then to the southernmost villages that local pastors had chosen for the ministry. Over the next three weeks, we, the Biola team, partnered with local pastors to present the biblical narratives of Adam and Eve, of Cain and Abel, and of Abraham and Isaac. Each of the stories emphasized the terrible cost of sin, and God's requirement of a blood sacrifice to atone for the sins of the people. We concluded the series with the stories of the ministry, death, and resurrection of Jesus. Local people heard these narratives in the vernacular, and the team members provided a visual role play picture of the story for the people to see and comprehend. None of the students were actors, and their role playing was at times puzzling and often hilarious to our African audiences. Yet each day the people came to hear the stories. At the end of the five days, one hundred twenty-three people responded to the invitation of the pastors to receive Christ or to renew their commitments.

For the local pastors, the Biola students, and for me, this ministry was a success. The pastors sent one of the narrators of our biblical stories to live in one of the villages to establish a local church for the whole area. The Biola students went home with glowing accounts of their ministry. In my convocation address to the Biola student body at the beginning of the spring term, I told the story of this wonderful journey with Biola students and God to the whole student body. And then, very quickly, the administrative challenges of the university filled my life, and pushed Chad and the ministry team from my personal agenda.

The Default Habit of Task Focus

From the perspective of twenty years later, God clearly blessed our ministry, but it is also clear that two of my vision and prayer goals for this ministry were not met. I failed to recruit any students for long-term mission; in fact, I walked away from them completely when I resumed work at Biola. And, we failed to impact in any way the vision of Chadian pastors for youth ministry. I have asked myself, what was my role in perhaps limiting this ministry impact? To answer that question, I then reflected on how I spent my time in preparation for and following that ministry, assuming that the time invested is a reasonably accurate reflection of my priorities.

The results of this reflection were sobering for me (see table 8.1). In retrospect, it is clear that two activities consumed most of my time prior to the actual ministry in Chad: first, screening candidates for the drama through the weekly prayer meetings, early morning bicycle rides, and prayer activity, and second, writing, preparation, and rehearsal of the dramas. In my ministry vision, planning and execution, I defaulted to *task focus—drama evangelism*, and failed to spend any time in dialogue with students about their long-term ministry goals, and reflection on possible careers in mission. I spent one hour preaching to Chadian pastors through an interpreter, and hoped that their seeing the narratives performed would be "catching." We used some Chadian youth as interpreters in the capital city, and had fellowship with them, but none were included in any aspect of the village ministry. And, while I believed and hoped our ministry would have some long-term impact, this was not something that I focused on at any time in the journey. I assumed that if we told these Bible stories, that my goals would be achieved.

TABLE 8.1 Chad Ministry Goals, 1997	
Goal	*Drama Evangelism*
Means	Prayer, Team Selection
	Prepare Dramas, Rehearse
	Select Location, Recruit Support
Ends	Decisions for Christ
	Mobilize Chad Pastors, Youth
	Recruit Men for Career Mission

The most important lesson I have learned from this reflection is that you achieve precisely what you have planned in accordance with your investment of time and energy. The dramas went well, the coaching and mentoring I did with students before, and in Chad, had a significant impact on them at that time, and two men have become lifelong friends. These men and women grew emotionally, spiritually, and culturally during the three weeks in Chad. They learned what it meant to suffer, and also to share in the suffering of others. They gained new insights into the cost and pain of poverty and life without Christ. And God spoke through their presentation of his word, and many people came to Christ.

However, my *task focus* on the drama ministry was a lesser goal, a lesser good; I completely missed the point that God had brought these men and women into my life so that I might help them to mature as disciples of Jesus Christ. I lost sight of the fact that *they* were the ministry for me, and that the drama was the *means* to bring them together and to help them in their walk with Christ. My most grievous action was to walk away from them when we returned to Biola. That was the time when many, if not all, needed my love and listening the most. My excuse was my all-consuming job, chief academic officer at Biola.

Learning a Covenant-with-God Focus

As I look back at this year in my life, I have gained some critical new insights. My calling in Christ is to follow him, and his work was/is always to glorify the father who sent him. Because of Christ, I serve in a new covenant relationship with God (Heb 10:15–25) such that my primary goal must always be to do the will of the one who sent me. I have learned to begin my next challenge by asking, up front, what are God's priorities for any short-term or long-term ministry? Have I searched the Scriptures to confirm what I sense the Spirit is saying to me? What priority should Jesus's command to "make disciples" have in my planning? How willing am I to listen (to pastors, youth) to see if this ministry vision is shared by anyone else, and if not, why am I giving it serious consideration? Once I have the answers to these questions, then I am ready to plan how I invest my time accordingly (see table 8.2).

Since we are part of a global body, I believe that the Spirit would lead me to ask how I might do *mission with* by partnering with God's servants in that place (Chad), and how I should invest in building that partnership with love, mutual respect, and resources. Then I must intentionally think and pray about priority and time to invest in the discipling and mentoring of others (students, Chadian pastors), and then about our opportunities together for ministry. The tasks are still an essential part of the work, but they have become the means, and secondary to God's agenda for the ministry.

TABLE 8.2 Reframing Chad Ministry Goals, 2017	
Goal	Glorify God: Mission "with" and Making Disciples
Means	Prayer, team selection, two-year commitment
	Listen, dialog with Chad pastors re: vision, location
	Prepare dramas, rehearse, engage Chad youth
Ends	Decisions for Christ
	Dialog re: next steps, mission with Chad pastors
	Mentoring students re: God's calling

Rehearsing the Covenant-with-God Focus

Even as I was writing this chapter, I was reminded of how quickly I default to my old habits. At that time Judy and I were planning to leave Pasadena for six weeks on two short-term ministry commitments in Indonesia and India. My default pattern had been to look at all of these commitments as tasks to be done, and a schedule of time to be allocated in my busy "retired" life. It became clear to me that, if I am not intentional and careful, I will repeat the habits that guided my preparation for the ministry to Chad. I will forget that these ministries are all about God's covenant relationship with me, in Christ, to be his servant for the mission of his church.

To break these default habits, we began by listening to the Holy Spirit and asking, why have you brought these particular opportunities into our lives at this time? How might we serve you with the gifts you have given to us in each of these ministry contexts? Our second challenge was to listen carefully to the people who had invited us to serve. What was the Holy Spirit saying to them (all) that led them to invite us to serve at this time? How was this specific calling related to God's mission for the community that they (all) are serving? How do we work together to bring glory to God, and to encourage and exhort people to follow us as we together follow Christ?

As we intentionally set aside time to pray and reflect on our goals for these ministries, we both experienced a subtle shift in our thinking away from the tasks and support structures for the short-term ministries, which had preoccupied us at the beginning. We both had felt ambivalent about teaching through translation in Indonesia, and wondered why our host had asked us to come. As we listened carefully, we heard more clearly that our presence was more important than our performance. Our colleague, working with a limited faculty, needed two more professors with PhDs to adequately support this ministry program. The class included advanced graduate students who were key leaders in dynamic growing ministries. Our contribution was more about being God's servants, speaking into the lives and ministries of these gifted national leaders, than professors teaching specific course content. Once we had this clearly in mind, we agreed to teach courses on technical subjects as a means to the larger purpose God had for our ministry there. And since we each had been mentor to the missionary colleague who was now the key faculty member in this program, we knew that God was calling us to continue to support and encourage that colleague.

Once we had a clear understanding of God's goal for us in Indonesia and India, beyond the learning outcomes for our classes, we prayerfully began the preparation that we needed to do, allocating our time and resources according to the goals that God had given to us. The most important thing that happened occurred in our prayer life. We began to pray for the leaders who had invited us, and for the work God was calling all of us to do to shepherd the flock that God had entrusted to them. We understood our task as part of the body of Christ in each area, partnering together for God's mission in those respective communities. Our course preparation, an essential part of the work, was now about being ready to serve our Lord in ways that would bring glory to his name. We were mentally and spiritually prepared for the challenges and surprises that came in both locations as we sought to honor his name.

We returned from Indonesia and India at the end of February 2015 with gratitude and joy about the ministries that God had given to us. In both places, Judy taught a graduate seminar on qualitative research methods and I taught a graduate seminar on cross-cultural leadership, but we understood from the beginning that these courses were the *means* and not the primary purpose for our ministries there. In each place God reinforced for us the need to listen carefully, to learn what God had been doing in the lives of these men and women before we arrived. We also understood that our primary task was to honor the Lord and to bring glory to God in whatever the circumstances of our living, teaching, and relationships.

We taught our courses, graded our papers, and contributed to the academic mission of each institution, but our best memories are those moments when we watched the Holy Spirit speak in fresh ways to them and to us. In retrospect, we understood why God had brought us to these places; as members of one body, we together grew in grace and the knowledge of our Lord and Savior, Jesus Christ. We were flourishing together in his service.

The fact that Judy and I successfully refocused for our ministries for Indonesia and India does not guarantee that we will do it again. In fact, every morning when I get out of bed, my default habits of a lifetime have awakened with me. To break the grip of such habits, we collaborate together to cultivate new habits that interrupt and defeat the old ones. In the chapters that follow, I will continue to reflect on the case study of the short-term drama ministry to Chad as a "window" through which we can understand and interpret biblical principles and apply them in the practice of reframing our leadership so as to flourish in church and mission ministries.

Reflection Questions:

1. What habits in my life led me to miss the call and opportunity to disciple the Biola students who participated with me?

2. Reflecting on how much time you invested in preparation, make a short list of the priorities that shaped your most recent team ministry.

3. In retrospect, whose priorities do you see most evident in that list?

4. How would you articulate the difference between ministry as goal and ministry as means to God's goal?

9

Leadership: It's about the "Body of Christ"

The power of the church, mission organization, para-church ministry or a theological seminary is directly related to its capacity to function as one body; when the people of God work together in the "unity of the Spirit," they have the capacity to attain "the whole measure of the fullness of Christ" (Eph 4:13). This is the second critical corner post, a pillar for our spiritual house that cannot, must not, be neglected. In Christ we are able, as a body, to do greater things than Jesus did in his ministry on earth. He promises this to those who abide in him, and unite together to do his work. Therefore, what does this mean for a pastor(s) role in God's mission for the church? A Latino pastor, Marti, comments:

> I am not the "role" I have at my church. This is easier to say than to act on it. Every time someone calls me pastor, indirectly [she/he] is recognizing authority and power when in a reality, I am just another person that is part of the body of Christ. He is the head and I am just his servant and my identity in Him is not based in my title as pastor, but is based in what He did for me on the cross.

Every pastor and ministry team faces the potential conflict of identity in leadership; who are we—the role that people attribute to us, or a person like the others, redeemed by the blood of Jesus, and now part of the body of Christ? When we merge our role with our true identity, we experience emotional and relational distress when people around us become displeased with our leadership, or we with their followership. The same is true for other members in the body—elders, deacons, teachers, evangelists, and serving parishioners are first and foremost formed as new creations in Christ Jesus. As such, our calling and roles are gifts from God, for the purpose of his church and his kingdom coming on earth through the church. Since we are all members of one body, and our identity is focused on Jesus Christ, we know that God's pleasure is not in the role we as individuals play, but rather when "the whole body, joined and held together by every supporting ligament, grows and builds itself up in love, as each part does its work" (Eph 4:16).

It's Not about the Most Gifted or Powerful

In Euro-American cultures we worship the most gifted people in our societies. This worship is seen in sports, the arts, history, and politics. In the Olympic Games, individuals and teams compete for the gold medal, and those who achieve them receive the worship of the media, and their nations, communities, families, and teammates. In the fine arts, we give glory to the most prominent actors and dancers, the most gifted musicians, the best-selling authors, and the artists whose works are so highly valued that only the wealthy can afford them. In professional athletics, we pay gifted athletes salaries that far exceed the salaries of medical doctors, university presidents, public officials, and even the president of the United States. In business, the CEO's of major companies are paid even more than professional athletes, their value measured by the performance of their companies in global competition for market share and the value of their stock.

And inevitably, people bring these same values with them into the church, so much so that thousands flock to mega-churches that have outstanding musicians leading worship, the most exceptional preachers, and the best professionals leading children's and other ministries. And the testimonies of professional athletes, and other prominent people are often highlighted in our fellowship and worship services.

What does Scripture say about professionalism in the church? In 1 Cor 12:21–23, the Apostle Paul writes:

> The eye cannot say to the hand, "I don't need you!" And the head cannot say to the feet, "I don't need you!" On the contrary, those parts of the body that seem to be weaker are indispensable, and the parts that we think are less honorable we treat with special honor. And the parts that are unpresentable are treated with special

modesty. Every part is essential to God's mission—to each one of us grace has been given as Christ apportioned it.

The body of Christ is analogous to an iceberg, the mass of which floats deeply under water, unseen to the human eye. The parts of the body that are visible, catching our attention, are only a small portion of the total body, and the power and strength of the body resides in its invisible parts, from which flows its capacity and power for the work of ministry. For example, the hands are nearly always visible, but a hand is helpless without the arm and shoulder, and the muscles and ligaments which give the hands their mobility and strength to work.

As Christian leaders, we know that every ministry is dependent upon God's provision of funding to do the work, and we also know that funding largely comes from the hidden parts of the body as the Spirit moves God's people to give. Yet in spite of that, we sometimes follow our culture, and honor the prominent donors, and fail to treat the hidden parts with special honor.

The fundamental lesson for leadership here is that "body work" is countercultural. It is not about structure, role, and rules. Rather, our most important functional role is made clear in Ephesians 4:16; the most visible spiritual gifts—apostles, prophets, evangelists, pastors, and teachers—serve as supporting ligaments, so that the body grows, and that every part does its work. This truth is so important, yet so counter to most cultural understandings of leadership. We prefer structure, roles, and rules. In the United States, congregational church members hire leaders so they don't have to do the work. In European state churches, the state becomes the authority for church work and polity, the ministers are the employees of the state, and the congregation has little if anything to do with ministry. In Korean churches, leaders and elders typically operate by command/control, and congregations follow the direction of either powerful founding pastors or a group of ruling elders; the members in these congregations are servants, and they do as they are instructed by those in authority over them. The leader who seeks to transform the local cultural system into "body work" as presented in Paul's epistles is rare, yet this is God's spiritual framework for leadership, to enable leaders and congregations to follow the way of Christ, the head of his church.

It's about the Body at Work

As I reflect Paul's teaching about the body in Ephesians, I have three questions: What are the works of service for which we are equipped? What is the purpose of "works of service" in the body of Christ? And finally, what does God envision as the result of the body at work?

What are the works of service? Paul is clear, Jesus Christ is the head of the church, and everything we do flows from him. Therefore, we turn to the words of our Lord to answer this first question. In the conversations during and after the Last Supper, recorded only in the Gospel of John, Jesus explains this work. After Judas is sent out to betray him, Jesus turns to the others and declares, "Now is the Son of Man glorified, and God is glorified in him." This is the time when Jesus will complete his sacrifice, the kernel of wheat dying to bring forth fruit. He declares that his disciples will be left behind, that they cannot come with him. But instead, he gives them a new command, "As I have loved you, so you must love one another. By this everyone will know that you are my disciples" (John 13:34).

At this point, Jesus knows these men are stunned, confused, and grieving. He is leaving, one is to betray him, and he declares that they will all abandon him and run away. Knowing that his crucifixion will be a period of darkness for them, Jesus reminds them that he is the light and if they put their trust in him, they will become children of light, strong in the midst of darkness. Jesus also speaks to their doubts and anxious hearts. He says, "Believe me when I say that I am in the Father and the Father is in me; or at least believe on the evidence of the works themselves" (John 14:11).

And then in John 14:12–13, Jesus gives this incredible promise: "Very truly I tell you, all who have faith in me will do the works I have been doing, and they will do even greater things than these, because I am going to the Father." This promise makes it very clear: we, the members of his body, will do the same works of service that he did.

What is the purpose of these works of service? As with all forms of exercise, it is focused first to build (increase?) and to strengthen the body. But even more importantly, through its work "the body of Christ may be built up until we all reach unity in the faith and in the knowledge of the Son of God and become mature, attaining to the whole measure of the fullness of Christ" (Eph 4:12–13). The glory of the Father is the ultimate purpose, and that is through Jesus, and his body, the church. As the body works, so is the Son glorified: "And I will do whatever you ask in my name, so that the Father may be glorified in the Son. You may ask me for anything in my name, and I will do it" (John 14:14).

What does God envision as the result of the body at work? The answer to this question is found in the larger context of Paul's letter. The first is transformed lives for the members of the body, no longer living in darkness, but instead clothed as new persons created in God's image of justice and holiness (4:17–24). The second is that members imitate Christ by putting on compassion, kindness, and forgiveness, living a life of love and light that produces the fruit of goodness, justice, and truth (4:29—5:9). The third is that members of the body be filled with the Spirit in order to worship together, to give thanks to God for everything, and to submit to one another out of respect for Christ (5:15–21). And the last is that members of the body stand as warriors of the faith, girded with God's armor, and joining together to spread the good news of peace (6:10–15). In the chapters that follow we will examine in greater depth the nature and character of works of service, and the practice of leadership through works of service.

Case Study: Drama Ministry in Chad

When I went to Chad in 1996, I did not understand the concept of "adaptive challenge," and the necessity of vulnerability for flourishing. But in retrospect taking a group of undergraduate students to Chad to do evangelism through story and drama was clearly an adaptive challenge. In the beginning, I received much encouragement from the mission board and home office of which I was part, and great enthusiasm from students at Biola. However, when I contacted the mission team on the ground in Chad, they were less enthusiastic. They were concerned about many issues, not the least of which was my ambition to go to an unreached Muslim ethnic group. Further, when they asked the local pastors about going to an unreached Muslim area, they declined and offered other suggestions. After some long-distance correspondence that surfaced value conflicts about the appropriateness of youth and ministry, story as preaching, and evangelism by truck or bicycle, we agreed to listen to one another—an act of vulnerability—and frame a joint plan for mission with one another.

The local pastors would select the specific people group for the evangelistic outreach, and provide the pastoral team to accompany us. The Chad mission team would facilitate transportation, housing, food, and the purchase of bicycles. I would recruit and train the student ministry team, prepare the drama stories with the help of both mission and Biola colleagues, and the international mission office would help us raise support and manage the visa, travel, and finances for the ministry.

Very early in this ministry I realized that it was not about my imagined or real role as one called and sent by God for this mission; rather, given the complexity of the work, and conflicting ministry and cultural values, I was excessively dependent upon others in the body of Christ. I focused on the work of prayer, calling, preparation of dramas, and performance, while Peg, my assistant at Biola, kept me connected to the students and supported me in every way. Sharon was knees for the team, catalyst for prayer, always there, but did not make the journey to Chad. Judy, my wife, was partner in every part of the preparation, hosting students in our home, coaching in drama rehearsal, and supporting us in all the logistics.

The Encompass mission team did all of the heavy lifting: Blaine—the "ligament" in Indiana—guided and supported us in all the details of visas, travel, support raising; Barb, veteran missionary, wrote the English version of the five stories for the drama ministry; Tom—the "ligament" in Chad—translated the French into Laka, brought Chad pastors together to select the villages and the supporting pastors for evangelistic outreach, and then coordinated all of the local transportation and arrangements. All of these worked in relationship with others who made their contribution possible.

And then the huge iceberg of families and friends encouraged, supported, and even opposed members of the team. One grandfather, a retired military officer, asked with respect why I would consider taking college youth, and his grandson, to such a challenging place. To him this was clearly a job for professionals. Scores of others and their congregations gave financial support to these men and women for this ministry, otherwise it would not have happened.

As I look back, this ministry journey was only possible because of a living body so large that I would never be able to see and thank all of the parts. The members of the team who persevered and went to Chad were not the most gifted or promising students at Biola—rather they were chosen by the Holy Spirit during months of prayer. The supporting ligaments included many gifted people at Biola, Encompass, and in Chad who made the whole ministry possible. And my role was not some bold visionary leader, but rather one of the many supporting ligaments that God was using to enable all in the body to do the work that Jesus had done before us.

Unity and Equipping Are Essentials

Larry Osborne argues that unity is "the one thing that can't be left to chance." It must be our top priority; Jesus prayed for it (John 17), and Paul challenges us to make every effort to achieve and keep it in our ministry together. But what does unity look like? Many people, Christian and non-Christian, define unity in terms of uniformity of thinking and behavior. If another person doesn't see an issue the way I do, we must agree or we cannot work together or be friends. For some Christians, doctrinal uniformity is a requirement for fellowship and ministry, and some would interpret the text above as demanding such uniformity. Osborne observes, and I agree, that a "unity that insists on uniformity isn't unity at all. It's a cheap counterfeit."[1]

Therefore, the challenge of adaptive leadership in church, mission, and seminary is to ask, how do we, God's apostles, prophets, evangelists, pastors, and teachers, for this moment in the history of his church, put into practice Paul's admonition to "make every effort to keep the unity of the Spirit" (Eph 4:3), so that each part of the body does its work? I have written that "the first characteristic of leading is building trust within a relational community,"[2] and that was a key priority for me in preparation for the ministry in Chad. It was clear that my desire to go to an unreached Muslim community was not shared by local pastors; I gave the choice back to them, and they chose a "resistant" community on their southern border. My missionary colleagues, Tom and Franck, challenged my ideal of working exclusively with bicycles, and we agreed to use bicycles and a truck. My Biola team did not know each other, and did not have any grounds for trust—we worked on that from the beginning to the end of the ministry. Trust follows when we listen to one another, learn from one another, and then we together frame the work that God has given to us to do.

Second to unity is the priority "to equip his people for works of service, so that the body of Christ may be built up"—this admonition has nothing to say about ministry success; equipping is not about performance or results, but it is rather all about building the body "in the faith and in the knowledge of the Son of God" (Eph 4:12). I confess that I spent more time working for successful performance of drama evangelism, than in equipping team members to be followers of Jesus. Each member of the student ministry team had stories of brokenness in their walk with Jesus, but I did

---

1. Osborne, *Sticky Teams*, 29.
2. Lingenfelter, *Leading Cross-Culturally*, 16.

not ask to hear those stories. I did not probe about habits of life that might be stealing their affection for Jesus. For me equipping was about preparation for performance of drama evangelism in Chad, and in retrospect, a grievous missed opportunity.

Leadership in the Body at Work

The ministry game—worship, witness, discipleship, church planting—is about every individual in the body working together, each giving their best effort, to achieve the game plan and the glory of God! The team captain, the head, is Christ, and "from him the whole body, joined and held together by every supporting ligament, grows and builds itself up in love, as each part does its work" (Eph 4:16). Out of this profound truth, the role of the ministry leader is not "head," but rather "supporting ligament," and the work is not about the performance of the leader or of the body, but about Christ.

The power of Christ in our ministries is unleashed by love; if one individual slips or fails another may step into the gap. If one individual is hurt, another is ready to do that work. When the game plan fails to achieve the goal, the ligaments and members of the body adapt to the unexpected challenge. The ministry work is always the means of building up the body, and never the end.

Love and growth flows from Christ. The work of ministry—the means by which we are the body—brings us together for God's purpose. The supporting ligaments enable each part to do its work. Body work is about composing ministry with the body and performing by the body for the glory of God. The end is the glory of God, and we become mature, attaining to the whole measure of the fullness of Christ.

Reflection Questions:

1. What surprises do you find in this chapter about the nature of Christ's body and its work?

2. In chapter 4, I described four distinctive structural types of denominational leadership; how does the metaphor of "Christ's body" challenge the assumptions of each type?

3. Discuss the tension between our cultural thinking about leadership and biblical teaching about Christ's body, spiritual gifts, and the body at work.

4. If we understand ministry as body work, how must this change our thinking, leadership, and the work of ministry?

10

His *Word*—Our Authority, His *Weakness*— the Way of the Cross

In Ephesians 2:11–21, the Apostle Paul employs a series of metaphors—one body, fellow citizens, members of his household, holy temple, and "a dwelling in which God lives by his Spirit"—to describe the "new humanity" reconciled to God by the death of Jesus on the cross. Paul employs these metaphors to correct the false assumptions and false teachings among the people in Ephesus about the cultural divisions endemic to the social structure in that city, and to the attitudes of some believers about the division between Jews and Gentiles. At the center of his argument is "the blood of Christ. For he himself is our peace, who has made the two groups one and has destroyed the barrier, the dividing wall of hostility, . . . His purpose was to create in himself one new humanity out of the two, thus making peace" (Eph 2:14–15).

Dividing Walls of Hostility

Unfortunately, humanity has not changed dramatically since Paul's day. In 2016, Western European nations were shaken by a flood of refugees fleeing from Syria and Iraq, and they were deeply divided about how to respond to this crisis. Some have been generous, and welcomed thousands of refugees, others have built fences and created laws to exclude or deport these people. All have divisions within their populations about how to respond. Europe itself is divided by two thousand and more years of language and cultural hostilities, in spite of the fact that these people and nations have been the heart of Christendom for more than one thousand years. And the United States, which is populated largely by immigrants from these European nations, took a hard stand against assisting these refugees.

The history of European nations, and the church within them, is one of recurring wars within nations and peoples that claim a Christian identity, and continuing hostility toward Jews. The Orthodox Church in Russia and Eastern Europe supported mass persecution of Jews in the nineteenth century and earlier. The Catholic and Protestant churches in Germany and the United States watched passively as Hitler killed six million Jews in the holocaust of World War II. The dividing walls of hostility are not dead, but quite to the contrary can be found in every expression of the church and Christian ministries around the globe.

By their very human nature, people inhabit communities of the flesh, driven by the interests and desires of family, economy and culture. The hostility that surfaces between them is rooted in their competing identities, conflicted histories, economic interests, and values and habits of life and worship. Further, every local expression of the church is populated by such people, who though redeemed by the blood of Christ, continue to live and work in their communities of the flesh.

Earlier in chapter 7, I defined "adaptive challenge" as an issue rooted in value conflicts that defy known solutions and require adaptive work. Such issues have at their core the "dividing wall of hostility" that is the focus of these texts. It is clear that even though Jesus died to "put to death" this hostility, we as human beings refuse to lay down our weapons. Therefore, the shepherds of God's flock face the daunting task of learning and loving, before they can effectively mobilize God's people to engage and serve God's purpose in this conflicted and broken world. In this chapter, we explore further what the Scriptures teach about leadership in the context of conflicted interests, competing cultures, and God's mission for his church.

A Dwelling in Which God Lives by his Spirit

The countercultural message of Ephesians is that Christ went to the cross for Jews and Gentiles to "put to death their hostility," and "to create one new humanity out of the two, thus making peace" (Eph 2:14–18). And as we saw in chapter 9, this church is "one body," called and equipped by God's leaders for works of service in their broken and hostile worlds. The challenge then for the church is to frame an internal culture of ministry that enables its people to embrace this vision of one new humanity and to engage in the practice of ministry that overcomes the hostilities inherent in their social contexts.

In the introduction to chapter 8, I have argued that the Scriptures provide critical and essential biblical components for transformed cultures of ministry, and while the Scriptures do not reject the diversity in human cultures, it defines for all peoples the essential components, or "spiritual pillars," for each local and national expression of the church. Constructing this symbolic picture from the physical structures of buildings for human occupants, we may imagine a classical Greek structure of stone pillars and stone walls, or an African village house of wooden poles filled with wattle or mud-brick, or a modern American building of wooden posts and beams, all of which support a roof and walls that provide shelter from rain, wind, and sun for the people. Each type of building incorporates pillars or posts that serve as the structural bones of the house that enable it to stand and serve. We may then imagine what might be the structural bones of a spiritual house in which God will dwell.

Chapter 8 asserts that the first corner post or pillar of any local expression of the church must always have as its primary focus the "glory of God." The Scripture teaches clearly that God *builds* his church "with Christ Jesus himself as the chief cornerstone" (Eph 2:20), God *dwells in* this "holy temple," and God's purpose is to *declare his glory* among the nations (1 Pet 2:9). Chapter 9 proposes that the second corner post is "one body"—this metaphor supersedes all other expressions of church structure and leadership, and provides the paradigm for all ministries and leadership within the church.

I do not have the spiritual insight, wisdom, or authority to determine what all of the other spiritual pillars might be, but I am taking the risk here to propose six additional pillars, presented as pairs—word and weakness, fellowship and forgiveness, worship and witness—each of which reflects the tension between authority and vulnerability in the life, leadership, and ministry of our Lord Jesus Christ. I believe these spiritual disciplines or "bones" of communal life are essential to the formation of followers of Jesus and a community in which God would choose to dwell.

It is my contention that any culture of ministry must in some way embed these pillars, and the tensions between them, into their spiritual house in order for the community and its leaders to flourish in their obedience to their calling in Christ and walking in the Spirit. Without these pillars, we will find it impossible to be true to our identity as "fellow citizens with God's people and also members of his household" (Eph 2:19) and to "live a life worthy of the calling [we] have received" (Eph 4:1).

The Transforming Authority of Word

In John's gospel (1:1–3), we read that Jesus is the *logos*, the living Word of God. "The Word was with God, and the Word was God," and all things were created by him. From the writer of the Hebrews (1:3) we learn that this Jesus is the Son, "who is the radiance of God's glory and the exact representation of his being, sustaining all things by his powerful word." So how is it possible for us to imagine leading or following apart from him? To follow Jesus is the essence of our calling, and for that purpose he has given us particular gifts of the spirit; it is through the power of his Spirit that we are enabled to use those gifts, serving as "supporting ligaments" in his body, the church. Apart from his Spirit, we are powerless, and worse, we are certain to fail in our attempts to serve his people.

In the life of our Lord Jesus Christ, we find a pattern of living and leadership that is centered on the authority and power of the written word of God. From the beginning of his public ministry to his trial and crucifixion, Jesus repeatedly cites the Scriptures as the compass and authority for his actions, Scriptures that upend every temptation to take power on his relentless journey to the cross. In the synoptic gospel stories of how Jesus was led by the Spirit into the wilderness to be tempted by the devil, Jesus repeatedly states "it is written" to stop the power of Satan. And when the devil counters by quoting Psalm 91:11–12, challenging Jesus to show his power by throwing himself down from the pinnacle of the temple, Jesus answered him, "It is also written, 'Do not put the Lord your God to the test'" (Matt 4:7). Jesus, the living *word*, cites Scripture, the written word, throughout his ministry to support his authority, to validate his work, and to affirm his obedience to the Father. Marguerite Shuster speaks of the "mystery of word"—that in fact it does matter what we say, "because somehow a deeper reality is tapped. In some mysterious way, good or evil wishes verbally expressed, or perhaps even thought, reverberate through us and our universe."[1]

---

1. Shuster, *Power, Pathology, and Paradox*, 203.

So, how might "Word" transform our cultures and leadership? Jesus has demonstrated for us that memorized Scripture has a mysterious power against evil, and when we draw upon it, "word," infused by the Spirit of the "living word," provides an internal compass—a powerful defense against hungers, fears, and judgment of others, and clear external direction and purpose. "Word" provides the essential counterbalance to the pressures of culture to squeeze us into its mold. By making explicit the lesser goals that tempt us and the cultural values that hold us in their grip, we are able through word and grace to refocus our people and leadership toward the glory of God, the mission of his church, and the well-being and unity of his people as they work as one to fulfill God's mission.

The Transforming Weakness of the Cross

From the beginning of his public ministry, Jesus chose the countercultural way of weakness, the way of the cross. In the narratives of Jesus going up to Jerusalem (Matt 20:18–19), on the way to establish his claim as the messiah, he makes it very clear that "the Son of Man will be delivered over to the chief priests and the teachers of the law. They will condemn him to death and will hand him over to the Gentiles to be mocked and flogged and crucified. On the third day he will be raised to life!" Throughout this journey to the cross, Jesus quotes the Scriptures that direct his journey, "the stone the builders rejected has become the cornerstone" (Matt 21:42); "the Lord said to my Lord, 'Sit at my right hand until I put your enemies under your feet'" (Matt 22:44); "for it is written, 'I will strike the shepherd, and the sheep of the flock will be scattered'" (Matt 26:31).

> More profoundly, Jesus commands his disciples to follow in this way of weakness. His words, recorded in the gospel of John (12:24–26) make this message profoundly clear: Very truly I tell you, unless a kernel of wheat falls to the ground and dies, it remains only a single seed. But if it dies, it produces many seeds. Anyone who loves their life will lose it, while anyone who hates their life in this world will keep it for eternal life. Whoever serves me must follow me; and where I am, my servant also will be. My Father will honor the one who serves me.

After his resurrection, and his forgiveness and restoration of Peter, "Jesus said, 'Feed my sheep. Very truly I tell you . . . when you are old someone else will dress you and lead you where you do not want to go.' Jesus said this to indicate the kind of death by which Peter would glorify God. Then he said to him, 'Follow Me!'" (John 21:18–19).

Structure and Power or Word and Weakness?

The world is ever present, and pressing God's people to conform to its sociopolitical systems. We have seen in our reflections on leadership crisis how our reliance upon organizational structures and processes leads us to trust in self-direction and to use power to achieve our ends. Bolman and Deal suggest we operate from "structural frame" assumptions that have become endemic and habitual in our cultures of leadership.[2] Over time we develop default habits, including trusting in the technical solutions from our leadership toolbox to cope with difficult challenges. We know that as Christian leaders, this is misplaced faith, relying upon systems and self rather than upon the "living word." Shuster argues that we simply cannot "get beyond the seduction of the self. . . . We cannot fix our corrupt selves by means of our corrupt selves. The possibility of *radical* change can only come from outside ourselves—from what the Christian calls *grace*."[3]

Our cultures despise weakness—an excuse for poor work, a justification for work avoidance, an absence of passion for excellence, a lack of pride and self-worth. The people on welfare are lazy, the crippled and maimed are to be pitied, the homeless are in bondage to alcohol and drugs, lacking dignity and self-control. We praise and honor winners, the best and the brightest, and we ignore and forget those who fail to take the prize. And the great leaders are those who achieve great success—the largest churches, the largest market share in business, the championship trophies in professional sports, and the strongest military and economic powers among nations.

But in Christ, the pathway of vulnerability opens a door into freedom—from fear of guilt, of shame, and of loss, and into the light God's glorious presence. By choosing to follow Jesus in weakness, our faith and dependence upon God increases. It is no longer about our performance, but rather about the body working together. By accepting the limitations of vulnerability and weakness, we more readily turn to others in the body for wisdom, help, support, and collaboration. By acknowledging our weakness and serving in humility, we empower others in the body to serve in their weakness, and in humility to take responsibility for their part and

2. See Bolman and Deal, *Modern Approaches*, 32–62.

3. Shuster, *Power, Pathology, Paradox*, 204, emphasis original.

participation in its work. Together we experience freedom from the cultural pressures to perform, to succeed, and to achieve the right outcome, and together we give glory to God for the work that God does through our weakness.

Leading without Weakness: Case Study in Chad

I return again to the case study of my leadership, guiding a team of Biola students for drama ministry in Chad. In this chapter I examine the cultural and power issues that produced "dividing walls of hostility," and reflect on my leadership by applying these two supporting pillars of any spiritual house, "word" and "weakness."

The mission of Encompass World Partners began in Chad in the 1950s. By 1997, the leaders of these churches—*Ecclesia Évangélique des Frères*—were among the most dynamic in Central Africa for church planting. Men equipped by both a mission funded Bible School, and by church planting workshops by local evangelists, had led the most rapid expansion of Encompass churches in Francophone Africa. This very rapid expansion made the cultural context of the Biola drama ministry in Chad even more complex than that of Europe and America. First Chad has over two hundred ethnic and linguistic groups among nearly fourteen million people, and approximately 55 percent are Muslim. The Encompass churches in 1997 included at least five different language and ethnic groups, and several factions of rival Chadian church leaders. These leaders and the mission had contested interests over limited mission and church resources, and ministry objectives.

After our village ministry, the pastors, missionaries, and the Biola student team traveled to another Chadian village, which that year hosted their annual conference. Pastors, laymen, and women gathered from all five language groups, and the men and women of the host district provided shelter and food in local homes and churches for the whole conference. The language of communication was French and Laka, a trade language.

Our Biola team attended the conference to share the drama ministry with all the churches represented, and to encourage church leaders to consider mobilizing their youth in similar ministries of their own. Over two days the team and supporting Chad pastors presented all five drama stories to an audience of nearly 1,500 people. The conference moderator then invited me to speak to the whole conference, during which I challenged them to consider such ministry with their youth, and offered them the drama materials in French and Laka. We had prayed and hoped that the pastors would take this tool and use it with their own young people to spread the gospel to unreached peoples through the nation of Chad.

The Way of the Cross or the Way of Power?

As I reflect on my leadership, I trusted my position and power to influence them. At the end of the conference many pastors told us that they had been moved by the dramas, and said they accepted my challenge. Some even asked if we could give them copies of the text so that they, too, could tell the stories in living pictures. But in retrospect it did not happen.

I had come with committed young people and the powerful story of the gospel, but, I was a stranger to them. I had a position of power in a distant place, but no relationship to them, and nothing to contribute to their ministry interests and priorities. I falsely assumed that presentation of the dramas, and a sermon challenging them would provoke change; I failed to engage them on any of their critical issues.

Leadership factions were the background noise for the whole conference, and ultimately that noise diluted and undermined the work of the Holy Spirit among them. One man and his followers walked out of the conference on the evening after the second cycle of team dramas; and rumors and gossip spread like fire through leaders and people alike during the closing day. The Biola team drama was entertainment, and perhaps spiritually moving to some in the crowd, but the factional noise of disunity drowned all else that transpired.

Instead of focusing on the blood of Christ to reconcile them as one body, they—leaders and people—fought over power issues: who should be the principal of the bible school, and who should be the moderator of the next conference. They did not focus on their common identity and mission in Christ, but rather on which leader and language group would be the greatest in the conference.

Word and Body or Command/Control?

I failed to see that bringing change of any kind to these church leaders was an adaptive challenge for me and for them, which required significant new learning on my part. The inherent value conflicts between us could not be solved by a sermon and a model ministry. The dramas were a "technical solution" offered and rejected by these very committed people, who had their own very viable and effective practices for evangelism.

I failed to understand the wide relationship gap. I had no relationship with these people, either personal or spiritual. I was an outsider, and a total stranger. They may have heard about me from my missionary friends, Tom and Franck, but this did not and could not build trust. Trust only comes through listening to one another, loving one another, and sacrificing for one another in God's mission.

And, I had a huge learning gap. I failed to do my homework on their leadership factions, their cultural values, and their ministry practices. I did not understand their concerns about age, training, and apprenticeship in preparation for ministry. I brought a group of young people who were seen as immature in their spiritual lives and service, and had the audacity to propose using such young people for the very important spiritual ministry of evangelism. I was blindsided by their ministry factions, and could not support or encourage my ministry colleagues because of my ignorance.

It was not possible to dialogue with these pastors about the role of youth in the mission of the church. I had not allocated time, and such a conversation required a much deeper commitment of time, trust and relationship than I was positioned or willing to make. To even have such a conversation required much more preparation in "word" and prayer. And to actually create the opportunity for conversation, I would have had to engage the youth of Chad with the Biola team in the drama ministry, and include more of the pastors in different locations as partners. In this I was completely naive.

Word and Weakness—Pillars in Our Spiritual House

Word and weakness are counterintuitive, they contradict the normative patterns of leadership in human culture and society. Whether in clans, kingdoms, or states, leadership is fundamentally about taking and exercising power for the goals of a sociopolitical system. I have commented earlier that the church lives within the tension of its indigenous structures and its life of pilgrimage in Christ, and the world is always pressing God's people to conform to its way.

In our ministry relationships in Chad, we together failed to see and hear the words of Scripture—one body, being built into a household of faith, a holy temple, a dwelling in which God lives by his spirit (Eph 2:10–22). Instead, we submitted to the "dividing wall of hostility." Our power-seeking and rivalry in the flesh, the noise of our arguments about leadership, and our in-group gossiping about the others drowned the voice of the Spirit among us and overwhelmed the power of word to unite us.

What if we had chosen to work from the way of Christ? At this point in time, we will never know, but clearly the way of the flesh did not accomplish God's larger purpose. As I look back at this opportunity, I often wonder what might have happened if I had chosen to follow Jesus in weakness, and take the time to listen, build relationships, and learn from these fellow servants of the Lord Jesus Christ. I wonder what might have happened if we had from the beginning planned a ministry that would include Biola students and Chad youth together as one body, working together to dramatize five gospel stories of sin and God's plan for redemption. I wonder how different the story might have been if I had begun the whole process by inviting Chad leaders to share their wisdom, help, support, and collaboration, framing the ministry as "mission with" rather than "mission to"?

What I can say with assurance is that my vision and plan for his ministry did not consider the body of Christ in Chad. In my self-assurance and pride, I thought I had something of value to give to them, and working in my strength, I gave an offering to the National Conference of *Ecclesia Évangélique des Frères* that the Lord could not and did not use as I intended.

I thank God that there was much more to this ministry than influencing pastors at the conference, and that God does his work in spite of our self-will and pride. In the following chapters I will share how in other moments of leading through word and weakness, we together presented an offering that was pleasing to God.

Reflection Questions:

1. What do you see in the Chad case about the cost of framing a cross-cultural ministry without a clear understanding of "dividing walls of hostility" in human cultures?

2. Why are we Western leaders so tempted to frame ministry as "mission to" rather than "mission with"?

3. What does Shuster's idea of the "mystery of word" suggest to you about framing our authority in ministry?

4. How would you explain to others the importance of weakness—the way of the cross for mission outreach?

11

Fellowship and Forgiveness:
Forging Bonds of Unity

The church is not structure, but people, and they are connected together by a spiritual unity derived from "one body and one Spirit, . . . one hope . . . , one Lord, one faith, one baptism; one God and Father of all, who is over all and through all and in all" (Eph 4:4–6). We know that Christ is the head of this body, and that he has given gifts to equip and support its members, working together in unity as every part does its work.

Marguerite Shuster suggests that unity of relationships within community is sustained by two virtues, fellowship and forgiveness.[1] These two virtues are absolutely essential to every spiritual house in Christ, they are pillars upon which the whole structure depends. The nature of the New Testament community of faith is captured in the Greek term *koinonia*. Luke used *koinonia* to characterize the "fellowship of sharing" with believers (Acts 4:32–33) and to describe Peter's relationship with James and John (business partners, Luke 5:10). Paul used the term in reference to suffering (*koinonia* of his sufferings, Phil 3:10), to the blood and body of Christ (*koinonia* in the blood of Christ, 1 Cor 10:16), and to describe to the partnership "in giving and receiving" that he enjoyed with believers at Philippi (Phil 4:15). Translators have translated this word *koinonia* as "fellowship" in the English language.

1. See Shuster, *Power, Pathology, Paradox*, 217–34.

Unity through Fellowship

If we understand culture and leadership within the church community as "body work," then the fellowship of sharing, of work, of giving and receiving, and of suffering is essential to knowing the body, with its gifts, strengths, weaknesses, distress, honor, pain, and joy. We must make time in our busy ministry lives for fellowship with one another. Such fellowship requires significant times of listening—learning to know one another, discerning the values, fears, hopes, and expectations of others. Larry Osborne relates how he changed his elder board meetings from business agendas to cultivating respect and friendship for this reason.[2] People who do not know and respect each other are not spiritually prepared to make decisions about the work of the kingdom of God.

Love is the core virtue for fellowship, grounded in the new command by Jesus "to love one another," and governing all relationships within the body of Christ. After Paul describes spiritual gifts and the "body of Christ" in 1 Corinthians, he follows with the greatest gift of all, love (1 Cor 13). Love covers all weakness, hurts, disappointments, fears, and wounds, and is the root source of kindness, gentleness, compassion, patience, and forbearance. If we commit these words to memory, and seek in the power of his Spirit to clothe ourselves daily with this love from Christ, our fellowship and leadership will reflect the glory that is Christ.

Shuster suggests that fellowship encompasses a willingness to suffer on behalf of members in the community of faith. Acknowledging that the source of suffering is essentially evil, Shuster asks, "How does redemptive suffering work?"[3] Citing Paul in 2 Corinthians 1:5–7, she suggests that sharing in Christ's suffering is normal for those who follow him, yielding both comfort and salvation to others in the community of faith. By bearing the pain and burdens of others, the one called to shepherd may become a source of healing within the community.

The Power of Forgiveness

What is the power of forgiveness? Leading and serving out of forgiveness is the most powerful expression of love. The word of Colossians 3:13 challenges us: "Bear with each other and forgive one another if any of you has

2. Osborne, *Sticky Teams*, 30–31.

3. Shuster, *Power, Pathology, Paradox*, 223–24.

a grievance against someone. Forgive as the Lord forgave you. And over all these virtues put on love, which binds them all together in perfect unity." In our congregations and communities, forgiveness is our source of healing power, a balm for angry souls and wounded spirits. When community relationships are strained by the pressures of performance, broken by the certainty of the "right way" of doing things, or crushed by guilt and shame, Christ's Spirit is present in us, teaching us to forgive, even as he has forgiven us, and restoring fellowship by his healing power.

How can a leader teach and shape a culture of forgiveness to build unity? We are diverse creatures, seeing and thinking in distinctive ways. We hold values that are often in conflict with values of others in our workplace, and we often insist that our way is the right way to do the work. We have hungers for control and significance, and when left to ourselves, these hungers lead to behaviors that destroy fellowship and overpower our fellow workers.

The first step in teaching forgiveness is to model repentance. Too often we excuse ourselves, "I did nothing wrong, but I am sorry for how you feel." One of my spiritual mentors has reminded me that the statement "I am sorry" is overused and ineffective. When people are wounded, they believe that "sorry" is a weak excuse, lacking genuine regret and repentance. It is therefore incumbent upon us that we be the first to say, "I was wrong," and even to explain why that is so; "I did not listen carefully," or "I judged," thus violating the Lord's command "do not judge." Once we have taken responsibility for the hurt, then we may follow with a request for forgiveness. It is obligatory for us to model this honesty and integrity, so that others in the body may see repentance in us and follow.

The most powerful act in teaching forgiveness is to practice forgiveness as Jesus has forgiven us, forgive people who in fact do not deserve to be forgiven. For a pastor who has been attacked by an elder, or threatened and abused by a faction of the church or board, this kind of forgiveness is extremely difficult. Usually people making such attacks justify them by an accusation that is wrong or unjust. Our immediate reaction is to fight back, and to return insult for insult. Defensiveness is the human response to such attacks, and leads to increased hostility and distance. Shuster suggests that such attacks are evil, people using will and power to obtain or control something of value to themselves. But she then points to the

Scripture—overcome evil with good (Rom 12:21), and she suggests that the only way to stop evil is to absorb it.[4]

In our three-week ministry in Chad, we had ample pressure and opportunities to criticize and even hurt one another. Students disagreed about music, bicycles, food, and the ways to play out our stories. Sometimes they expressed frustration with local people about behaviors that they did not understand or could not control. Without fellowship and forgiveness, a community fragments, and the factions that form begin to war with one another, undermining body work and destroying our joy.

Growing through Fellowship and Forgiveness in Chad

When my Biola team of six men and two women arrived in Chad, we discovered a whole new meaning of relationship. Yes, we had prayed together weekly during the past year, and the men and I had gone biking in twos and threes in the predawn of California winter, praying for Chad and this ministry. Yes, we had gathered on a beach for several Saturdays in November and December to rehearse how to role play the bible narratives for our ministry. But we had no idea of what it meant to live and work together on such a challenging journey for ministry in Chad.

The first crisis erupted our very first morning in Chad, as we gathered for worship after breakfast. We had carried with us a "boom box" and some music tapes to facilitate our worship together. After we finished singing and praying together, Gardner complained, "I just can't worship with that canned music!" Chris agreed and pulled out his guitar which he had carried on the flight from Los Angeles. After a short conversation together, we agreed to store the boom box at the mission center, and Gardner and Chris would lead us in our worship music for the rest of the journey.

However, in the hours that followed, as we struggled to rehearse the drama role play while our Chadian pastor narrated the first story of Adam and Eve, we learned that our language differences—English, French, and Laka—provided a nearly impossible barrier. While we had, with the support of Tom, the local American missionary, prepared drama texts in English and French and Laka, the team understood only English, and the narrator had to tell the story in Laka. After some intense discussions together, I found a way to be the language coach for the team, following the

4. Ibid., 250–52.

written Laka and French texts, and translating verbally into English at each critical moment in the story.

The very next day the team flew to the southern city of Moundou, and after one night there, we traveled south to the five villages located just north of the Chad border with the Central African Republic. At this point, the shock of living and working together in very challenging circumstances tested us in nearly every aspect of our relationships.

Suffering: Prelude to Repentance and Forgiveness

We expected to suffer in Chad, and it was for that reason several joined the team. As team leader, I had chosen 1 Peter 4:1, 7–11 with its focus on suffering, just before our departure as the text for reflection throughout our ministry. Nobody really knew what it meant to "suffer for Jesus in Chad" until we camped at Nzoro and began the daily trek of ministry. We expected the situation might be tough, but lacking experience we had no clue of what we would encounter. And the first two days of the ministry were especially tough.

We knew that Chad was a hot place, but we had no idea that it was also a cold place. The first night in the village where we were ministering most of the team slept outside and discovered that the one wool blanket each had was inadequate to keep out the cold from the night air coming down on us.

Sleepless nights resulted from close quarters, chilling cold, conversation of local guards sitting by a fire, and children beating on drums and singing beyond the midnight hour. And worse, it was fifty yards to the hole-in-the-ground toilet. We expected that the toilet facilities would be different. We didn't expect we would have to walk so far, and that there would be such little water for personal bathing. For those who were sick, fifty yards every half-hour during the night was no fun.

On our first day of drama ministry we had millet and goat for breakfast, lunch, and dinner. I remember at lunch time, one of the guys commented about intestines in the meat bowl. Hans said, "I can eat that," and he picked it up and plopped it in his mouth, chewing it up as if it were the choicest piece of steak. That evening he downed a few other tasty morsels that his teammates pushed his way. At about 9:00 pm he burst into the church where we were sleeping and said, "Dr. Lingenfelter, I feel sick. I ate everything today. I am really going to get sick. I feel terrible." At that moment, I reminded him of our prayer time that morning where Jesus promised us that he not only wants to answer our prayer, he begins to do it even as we ask. We then prayed about his nausea and we asked the Lord to settle his stomach and give him strength for the next day. I asked Hans if he really believed Jesus cared, and he said he knew he did. He went to bed and woke up well and strong the next morning. His fear of sickness was gone for the rest of the trip.

Sin was often at our door. Our sinful attitudes were expressed most frequently in our joking behavior. We were most discontent about the food. Our African hosts prepared and provided food for us three times a day, but it was the same morning, noon, and night—a mush made of the local grain "millet," and boiled goat stew. We made jokes about eating at Taco Bell, the Olive Garden, and some talked about holding a big celebration at Home Town Buffet. We were not thankful for the food, nor grateful to our hosts. In our hunger, most, if not all of us, at one time or another grabbed selfishly for the best pieces of meat in the pot. Some took more than their share. If we had the power, we would have surely turned the millet into pizza.

Soon a critical spirit spread like a virus through the team—sometimes we made jokes about the people, we made jokes about one another, and we often joked about the bikes. All of our jokes covered subtle resentments and rejection of one another and the local people. I was surprised at my own joking and realized that it was sometimes subtle criticism of team members. This was not the leadership to which Christ called me.

The Practice of Repentance and Forgiveness

By the third day of our stay in the village of Nzoro we realized that we were neglecting our focus on the Lord Jesus Christ. Several members of the team voiced a desire for a greater commitment to prayer, for collective worship, and for a renewal of our commitment to our purpose. We met that evening after the drama cycle, and we focused anew on our purpose for being there, to share the gospel of the Lord Jesus Christ. I reminded them of our ministry text in 1 Peter 4, and as we reflected and prayed together on that text, we experienced the freedom that Peter promises, "Therefore, since Christ suffered in his body, arm yourselves also with the same attitude, because whoever suffers in the body is done with sin" (1 Pet 4:1). Armed with the attitude of Jesus Christ, we resolved to be done with sin. By focusing on our commitment to share the gospel, we also renewed our commitment to "live according to God in the Spirit," and to "be clear minded and self-controlled so that you can pray" (1 Pet 4:6–7). This Scripture shaped our culture of ministry for the remainder of the journey.

Because we were stripped of nearly everything that made us comfortable at home, it was not difficult to be clear-minded about what was happening to us. It was more difficult to be self-controlled; so, we committed ourselves to submitting to one another, to giving ourselves to prayer, and we recited the admonition of 1 Peter 4:8, "Above all, love each other deeply, because love covers a multitude of sins." As we worked through the week we prayed for one another and continued to seek to love one another. Several incidents of love in action stand out in my mind.

We were the recipients of tremendous hospitality. Everywhere we went African believers greeted us with love, fed us the very best of their food, offered us their homes to sleep in, and responded to our every need. We never heard a grumble or complaint among them. Their spirit was infectious, and we found ourselves loving them and desiring to share our hospitality with them.

At the village where we camped each night, Hans, the bowels of mercy on the team, and Holly, the eyes, were particularly touched by a crippled and naked boy who came to the fire every evening. I noticed in the middle of the week that the boy had clothing. He was wearing shorts and a T-shirt that had been worn by Hans and Holly earlier in the week. Others on the team began to catch this spirit and soon were giving away a precious power bar, or a granola bar in spite of knowing that the only other alternative was millet and goat.

Later, in a team meeting in the city of Moundou, after our week of drama ministry in Nzoro, Ernestiene, the body's nose on the team who smelled a critical spirit, and Holly, the eyes, who saw their mocking behavior, shared their concerns and their observations. Together we identified some patterns of selfishness that had become part of our attitudes and actions. Brad, the feet on the team that kept things moving, spoke up in the meeting and said, "I did that, and I am sorry." His candid confession, and his acceptance of responsibility demonstrated his love for the team members, for the Lord Jesus Christ, and for the people to whom God had sent him to minister.

Each individual member spoke about his or her own attitude and need for confession and prayer. I also had some maturing to do, since I had lived and worked cross-culturally for thirty years and I was at times impatient with young people who somehow couldn't get it right. I didn't like my jokes, and I found myself being sharp and impatient with individuals on the team when they didn't see things my way. When I confessed this matter to the Lord and then to members of the team, I experienced their love and forgiveness. We talked together and we prayed together and the Lord healed our wounded spirits and renewed our commitment to him and to his mission for us.

Discerning the Spirit of Fellowship and Forgiveness

As is clear in the case study, these eight students came to Chad as individuals, acquainted with one another, and sacrificially committed to three intense weeks of ministry in Chad; but they were not a team, they did not share a culture of ministry, nor did they understand what it meant to work together as the body of Christ. In the very short time period of one week, they entered an intensive experience of *koinonia*, the fellowship of sharing, of work, of giving and receiving, and of suffering together. In the earliest days, their individualism and interests surfaced around particular aspects of ministry or personal living. They voiced these interests most frequently as a complaint or a cutting joke.

We, the team, had to suffer together before we were willing to submit to one another in Christ. That suffering was first through the shared misery of our unusual living conditions, but also in diverse and individual challenges to persons on the team. One bicycle failed more often than another; one person was afflicted with sickness more often than another. The "critical spirit" phase surfaced early, and lasted through that first week. However, I observed mutual trust forming through mutual suffering, and our response to surrender critical spirits in ministry and worship.

My role as leader was first to participate in their suffering—eating, sleeping, toilet, and even riding a bicycle with them; and then to listen, to love, to encourage and support them individually and as a group. I called them to prayer in the morning and the evening, and I did not preach or teach—instead we listened to the Lord through reading the word, we listened to what the Spirit was saying to each, we sang as the Spirit led us, and we prayed about our individual and collective needs. My work was to keep them engaged as the body, seeking together our unity in Christ.

Confrontation and confession were essential to fellowship; as I listened to the rumblings in the group, I intervened on two particular moments in the three weeks, creating the worship, confrontation, and confession moments to allow the Holy Spirit to speak to us individually and collectively. These moments were essential for our unity, and confession, repentance, and forgiveness moved us deeper in our relationships with Christ and with one another.

Over the three weeks of this ministry, hospitality—given and received—transformed relationships; one's gift to another, stimulated more giving and receiving, and this spirit spread from our hosts to the team, and then back. But most important, forgiveness broke the power of our critical spirits, and bound us together when the conditions of suffering did not change.

Reflection Questions:

1. Why did our collective suffering in Chad serve as a catalyst for unity?

2. What are the implications of the Chad story for unity in congregations and mission communities?

3. How would you go about building fellowship and forgiveness into your culture of leadership for your ministry community?

12

Worship and Witness:
God's Mission, Our Response

What do worship and witness have to do with leadership? It is common
to think about worship and witness as the products of leadership—
leaders plan and execute a worship service; musicians lead worship; worship is a timed event. Witness is also a program or a product—outreach,
evangelistic meeting, musical, short-term mission, or drama. As we have
seen earlier, we have drifted into cultural habits that distort God's plan
for his church. Product of any kind becomes a human agenda. My drama
evangelism ministry in Chad was clearly product focused—I had very clear
ends in mind—reaching unreached peoples, Bible story and drama, and
mobilization of youth and leaders in Chad.

Sunquist reminds us that worship and witness must be core values of
our corporate cultures and embedded habits of practice:

> The church, the body of Christ, has two basic purposes for its ex-
> istence: worship and witness. . . . A church that is not worshiping
> or is not working at worshiping with greater humility and joy has
> lost the empowering purpose of its existence. . . . As the church
> goes out in mission, it is the presence of Jesus Christ among the
> nations: loving, healing, including, proclaiming, and reconciling.
> . . . Witness without worship is a vain human invention. Worship

without witness is a deception, as if we are truly honoring God while we disobey his clearest and last command.[1]

Worship and witness are body work, activities in which the members of the body first come together in humility before God, and engage together in joyful listening to the Spirit of God through word, prayer and praise; from that worship, they then respond going out in their communities, testifying to the death and resurrection of Christ, and as Jesus's followers, doing the works that he did—healing the sick, serving the poor, and proclaiming the good news of the kingdom. Worship and witness are the Christian's active obedience to the two great commandments, to "love the Lord your God with all your heart and with all your soul and with all your mind and with all your strength," and to "love your neighbor as yourself" (Mark 12:30–31).

The argument of this chapter is that worship and witness are structural components, pillars, for any and every cultural expression of the church. Therefore, the challenge for leaders is to focus our will on God, rather than on our project agendas, and to build into our culture core commitments to worship and witness. While this may seem a simple task, our "will in the flesh" has an astounding vitality and assertiveness to distract us from a single-minded focus on God.

Worship—Refocusing Authority from Leaders to God

Worship begins with praise! Praise is first about God—the glory of his appearing; the beauty and marvel of creation; the wonder and mystery of his compassion and care for humanity; the gift of Jesus Christ to a lost and broken world; the wonder of the Scriptures and their testimony to God's care for and compassion to humanity. Shuster suggests, "We may truly thank and praise God for all that befalls us if we trust his purpose and know that he will not abandon us to situations more stressful than we can bear."[2] When we shift focus from ourselves, and our very local and often petty concerns, to confidence and hope in God's loving and unfailing presence, then gratitude and rejoicing flow from our inner being. Such confidence in a trustworthy God enables us to grant forgiveness when we are wounded, to offer healing help to others when we are hurting, and to give sacrificially in times of personal scarcity and distress. By trusting God in such situations

1. Sunquist, *Understanding Christian Mission*, 281–82.
2. Shuster, *Power, Pathology, Paradox*, 249.

of risk, we reap the spiritual fruits of endurance, character, and hope. In this shift, our self-awareness increases, we begin to sense our indebtedness to the creator of the universe, and our insignificance is magnified. Our response shifts from ordinary things to worship.

Prayer and praise together shift the focus from human authority—leaders, participants, and their decisions—to being in right relationship with God.[3] When a community gathers to pray, people inevitably come with their own personal fears and needs in focus; however, when prayer begins in worship and thanksgiving to God, participants may shift focus toward God, and many open their minds and spirits to God's spirit, and to listening collectively to God.

In all communities of faith, it is possible and probable that we leaders may seek to influence the minds of the participants toward our "ministry agendas." We have the work of ministry to do, and we have authority to oversee, and be sure that it is done. However, by genuinely seeking God on matters of critical importance to the community of faith, the focus of authority shifts—people may listen to God, rather than telling God what they fear, want or need. When this happens, power shifts from the leaders and the participants to the Spirit of God. As Sunquist says, as "we empty ourselves more and more in unbroken praise," God then empowers us through his Spirit for his work.[4]

In the Chad case study, I have documented my habit of framing a product-focused ministry and making the product the center of my time, energy, and commitment. True worship is the antidote to our ingrained habit of trusting our ability as leaders to motivate people to support our agenda, and to make things happen. Worship is focused on God, God's purpose and will for us as his redeemed people, and God's will and power to accomplish his purpose. In product-focused ministry, the players who produce the product get the glory and celebrate their victory; in worship-focused ministry, the prayers, players, and the victory all belong to God.

When we seriously believe that God is the source of all blessing for his church, mission and church leaders will then rethink about how to change the ministry culture from product to prayer agendas. This is not to argue that the realities of a congregation do not involve very important political issues. Leaders must be very aware of the dangers of factions, and of the reluctance of people to commit resources to resolve structural limitations

3. Ibid., 240.
4. Sunquist, *Understanding Christian Mission*, 281.

that are very real obstacles for effective outreach ministries. We must be very wise, listen carefully to people, and discern their anxieties and weaknesses. Unless God moves them to remove these obstacles, the risk of backlash and opposition is very great.

Witness: Worshipers at Risk for Proclamation

Witness is the essential work of the church, the manifest "presence of Jesus Christ among the nations: loving, healing, including, proclaiming, and reconciling." As Sunquist declares, "Worship without witness is a deception."[5] Yet, tragically, church members often make little or no connection between the body of people who gather for Sunday worship and the work of witness in a wider community during the week that follows.

Culturally we have embraced the notion that Sunday worship is a routine that is worthy of our time and energy, and even our offerings, but that same culture creates a sharp divide between weekend worship and weekday work. We may have heard that "the church is the only institution whose sole existence is for its non-members," but most have not been able to reframe our cultural thinking to take witness with us into the economic work week. A clear obstacle to witness is the American cultural divide between work and worship: we learn and are taught in schools and public media that our faith is a private thing, and there is much social pressure against those who are emboldened to witness in their workplace or the wider community. For many Christians, to act against this norm is a risk that they are reluctant to take.

Sunquist calls us to rethink and reframe our leadership culture and habits: "The church is the body of Christ, pointing to the Father, and living sacrificially for the sake of the world—a world that is still in rebellion."[6] If we are to grasp fully this calling to Christ's body, we must rethink everything we do in the body toward that sacrificial life and vulnerability of witness. This is not about program, or outreach activities, it is about changing the way we think about and live out the mission of the church. It is about renewing our commitment to God's purpose for his church, and then giving back to the people the work of rebuilding the life of the church for that mission.

5. Ibid., 284.
6. Ibid.

One of our first tasks is engaging the members of the body in the work of listening and attentiveness to their local context. Without careful observation and listening, we cannot see or hear where God is already at work. We do not know to whom God is already speaking and how then we might cooperate with his Spirit. We cannot hear the pain of those who are suffering and offer the healing touch of the Lord Jesus Christ. The work of attentiveness is perhaps the greatest weakness in our program-driven churches. This must be the prelude to all of our works of witness and service. And, when we have done that careful listening, we will proceed in ways that we could not have imagined in the beginning. My vision and ministry plan for Chad changed dramatically over the year we planned this ministry, primarily because we listened to our partners in Africa, who understood the ministry context, and refocused us on where and how best to serve God's mission for those churches.

To equip members of the body for the work of witness, we must intentionally bring people together in partnership for the ministry. Our mantra in the twenty-first century must be *mission with* those that God has already touched and called to this work. Such partnership may be between two persons, as Jesus practiced in sending his disciples into the towns and villages in Galilee. Urban communities may provide many other opportunities for partnership, and for many diverse kinds of ministry. A congregation that seeks to minister to the poor, the homeless, the jobless, and to prisoners have many possible partners in an urban context, and to minister together with the larger body of Christ has far greater impact than working alone or in pairs. And sometimes it is possible to partner with government or secular service organizations, when it is clear that we do not need to surrender our identity as servants of the Lord Jesus Christ.[7]

Above everything else, we must be clear that witness is about Jesus, the crucified Son of God, who through his death and resurrection offers us the forgiveness of sins, and the hope of resurrection with him for eternal life. This same Jesus offers comfort to those who mourn, healing to those who are physically or emotionally broken, and joy and peace to those have no peace. But most importantly, Jesus is the good news of hope and purpose for those who are lost and seeking direction, and he calls those who believe in him to follow him in a life of love and service.

To effectively mobilize the body for witness, we must be very clear about the cost. Sunquist is correct when he observes that "there is a

7. Ibid., 304–10.

cost to conversion and a cost to leading a person through the process of conversion."[8] To do the work of witness we must move out of our comfort into unknown territory—to fellowship with unbelieving people—students, workers, poor, prisoners, and anyone willing to hear good news. These are areas of significant vulnerability for worshipers: sacrifice of time, building new relationships, and changing our priorities in life, including our calendar. The work of witness involves dying to "security, comfort, relationships" for the purpose of sharing the gospel.[9] Unless we, as members of the body, are willing to go together in humility and to endure some deprivation of that which we enjoy and treasure, we will not do this work. As leaders, we must be honest about the challenge, and prepare our people for this level of commitment and readiness for the opportunity the Spirit will provide for us to accomplish God's purpose.

With gratitude to God I will now share with you the story of how God brought together as partners a multicultural team of pastors, missionaries and students for the work of worship and witness in Chad.

Witness: The Gospel Story in Five Villages

At about 7:00 am on January 6, 1997, six men mounted their bicycles and the two women, missionary men, the African pastors, and I rode a truck for a very rough ten kilometers to the village of Konne. When the truck arrived, the local chief greeted us, and sent messengers to call the people together. As the bikers trickled in, Tom, our mission leader, guided them to unload the sound equipment, and set up for the drama presentation.

At about 8:30 in the morning our Chad pastor-narrator told the story of Adam and Eve in the Laka language, and, with my coaching in English, the Biola team members provided a visual picture of the story for the people to see and comprehend. Following the Laka narrative, the second Chad pastor retold the story in the local Mbum dialect, so that women and children watching would understand, and he invited them to consider the meaning of this story for their families and community.

About 9:30 am we packed the truck, and returned 2.5 kilometers to village #4, where we set up the sound system, waited for people to gather, and then presented the story of Adam and Eve to these people in the same manner. Repeating this cycle in villages #3 and #2, we packed for the last

8. Ibid., 329.

9. Ibid., 330.

time and arrived in Nzoro, our camp village, about 4:00 pm, where we set up and performed the Adam and Eve story for the final time. Following this presentation, we gathered for prayer and thanksgiving to God for the day of ministry and we together committed the offering of our day's work to his Spirit.

Each day we repeated the cycle, and the people came. We told the story of Cain and Abel, and of Abraham and Isaac, emphasizing in each story the terrible cost of sin, and God's requirement of a blood sacrifice to atone for the sins of the people. On the fourth day, we dramatically portrayed the story of the birth and the ministry of the Lord Jesus Christ. The crowds loved Holly's portrayal of a pregnant Mary, Hans's portrayal of an exuberant leper who had been healed, Brad and Gardner's portrayal of the disciples tossed and fearful for their lives on the Sea of Galilee, and Tim and Hans's portrayal of the two demon-possessed men who met Jesus and the disciples in the region of the Gadarenes.

On the last day, we told the story of the crucifixion and the resurrection of the Lord Jesus Christ. As Chris played the role of Jesus, and as Kurtis and Brad beat him, kicked him, spat on him, and then bound him and nailed him to a cross, most of us watching had tears in our eyes, and the villagers watching laughed with their deep anxious laughter that characterizes moments of crises in which the outcome is certain to produce injury and even death. But the story did not end there, Ernestiene and Holly portrayed the joy of Mary and Mary Magdalene as they came to the tomb on Sunday morning to find the stone rolled away.

The last evening in the camp village of Nzoro the team worked with Tom to set up the *Jesus Film* to portray through another medium more of the story of Jesus that we had been telling on Thursday and Friday. More than one thousand people came, and only the Lord himself knows how many responded to his story.

Witness Builds Up the Body in Work

On Monday and Tuesday, it seemed that things fell apart. Some on the team had bad nights, unable to sleep because of the cold, or suffering from diarrhea with change in food and water. The men riding bicycles straggled into Konne each day, some riding, and two or more pushing bicycles that had broken chains or peddles. They all complained about the poor quality of these bikes, purchased at a local shop in Moundou. The drama presentation in Konne seemed awkward, and the coordination of narration and mime broken at best. No one was happy with the first performance. As we loaded equipment on the truck for the return trip to village #4, the broken bicycles were loaded, as well. However, by the end of that first day the repetition in five villages gave everyone more confidence. And when we arrived at Nzoro where we were camping, some local young men helped unload the broken bicycles and then, with old spare parts, to repair them.

By Wednesday afternoon, we had mastered the drama performances, but not the interpersonal relationships. At our lunch meal, the elder pastor rebuked the young men for grabbing the best pieces of meat, coaching them that the Chad way is for the young to wait for the elders, allowing them to reach first. Yet by the end of this day, it was clear that this diverse group of people—young and old, men and women, African pastors, missionaries and students—were reaching unity as the body of Christ. Very gradually over three days, as we together told stories of sin and God's plan of redemption five times each day, the Holy Spirit did this work among us. By the time we finished the story of how Abraham, in obedience to God offered his son Isaac, and God had provided a ram, we all understood God's son, Jesus, as the sacrifice on our behalf. We worshipped together than evening, and felt the Spirit of God move in our midst, lifting the frustrations of daily life and filling us with the joy of the Lord, so that we grew "in the knowledge of the Son of God."

Worship Builds Up the Body in Love

The worship of God is about the repetition of silence, word, prayer, praise, and thanksgiving. In this Chad ministry, there was much repetition. We had breakfast coffee, noon and evening meals together. While unity was slow to come on the first few days of our journey together, suffering together daily with cold water bucket showers, sleeping in local houses or under the stars, eating local food together, and bouts of sickness seemed to open our hearts to one another.

The most powerful piece, however, was telling the stories of the gospel—pastors, students, coach (me), and missionaries together—and at the end of each day, we knew that God had worked within and through us. We watched peoples' faces, we heard their laughter, we saw their responses when our pastors spoke to them about their relationship with God. We recounted daily what God had done in our evening fellowship together.

We prayed, and rejoiced together at both ends of each day. These were the moments when our work brought us to greater "unity in the faith and in the knowledge of the Son of God."

Our Wednesday evening worship was a "crisis" worship. We spent time together confessing our sins against one another. We remembered our complaints, and our frustrations with one another and with local people. We repented of our sins, asked God and one another for forgiveness, and it was at this time that we felt the Holy Spirit work in us, the body, to "build itself up in love."

We also took time to be thankful, especially for the local men who assisted the Biola men with broken bikes, and for the local women who were cooking for us each day, serving food to us and listening to our gospel stories. The little acts of kindness often had the most profound impact. We watched Tom, our missionary host, purify a large container of water using iodine tablets, and we realized how much loving care went into the planning by our missionary and African hosts to serve us there. And we listened as Tom translated for us the words of wisdom and encouragement from the two pastors who were our voices and ears to the local people.

Word, Suffering, Worship, and Witness

As I reflect on this ministry week with the Biola team, our listening to and meditation on God's word always brought us back on course. At the beginning of our journey, we meditated on 1 Peter 4:1–11, and we returned to that text repeatedly during the journey. When we were in crisis, fragmented in our relationships and work, we always returned to Scripture to guide us through. When we were afraid, we reflected on word and prayer, and the Spirit gave us courage and hope. At the end of the journey we remembered how God had guided us, and fulfilled his promises to us in that text, and we rejoiced.

The second essential factor in the growth of this body was suffering—as a ministry team we faced physical, emotional, and relational challenges. Crisis was the most important opportunity to lead us into deeper relationship with Christ; leaders who focus upon "kingdom" community know that the crisis is the golden opportunity to make disciples.[10] The Scriptures are very clear—suffering is the defining moment in the discipleship process. We turned repeatedly to the words of the Apostle Peter, "Therefore, since

10. Lingenfelter, *Leading Cross-Culturally*, 70–82.

Christ suffered in his body, arm yourselves also with the same attitude, because whoever suffers in the body is done with sin" (1 Pet 4:1). We also remembered the words of the Apostle Paul, "I want to know Christ—yes, to know the power of his resurrection and participation in his sufferings, becoming like him in his death, and so, somehow, attaining to the resurrection from the dead" (Phil 3:10–11). We are grateful that in this situation we found no quick solutions for our emotional and social pain, but rather by embracing the crisis as an opportunity, we together grew more mature as his body, and into a deeper relationship individually with Christ.

In our times of crisis, the team moved from grumbling and complaint to worship—repentance, prayer, and praise. These actions shifted the focus from our individual wants and needs, and decisions about self, to being in right relationship with God. Our growing confidence in a trustworthy God enabled us to grant forgiveness when we were wounded, to offer healing help to others when we were hurting, and to give sacrificially in times of personal scarcity and distress. By trusting God in such situations of risk, we reaped the spiritual fruits of endurance, character and hope, and gratitude and rejoicing flowed from our inner being. In this shift, our self-awareness increased, we begin to sense our indebtedness to the creator of the universe, and our insignificance was magnified. Our responses moved from the ordinary to worship.

Finally, witness brought us into a fullness of joy and expectation that only Christ can give—the gospel of Jesus Christ is glorious news, and sharing this gospel story with five villages made everything else insignificant. During the fifth day of the dramas, the Chad pastor gave an invitation in each of the five villages, and men, women, and children raised their hands to receive Christ. When, at the end of that day, our Chad pastors counted a total of 123 people who had made decisions to follow Jesus, nothing could have given us greater joy! Witness is the fundamental mission of God for his church!

Reflection Questions:

1. What place do worship and witness have in your culture of leadership?

2. Which of these two structural components of your spiritual house are in need of repair?

3. What stories can you find in your spiritual house about how the work of worship and witness have built up the body of Christ?

4. How might you tell these stories in such a what that others are inspired to follow?

13

Flourishing in "Jars of Clay"

> But we have this treasure in jars of clay to show that this all-sur-
> passing power is from God and not from us. (2 Cor 4:7)

The most challenging crisis of my years in academic leadership occurred in January of 1998. As the provost and senior vice president
of Biola University, I had appointed a dean of students in 1993 who had
been ordained an Anglican clergy, but had transferred his membership
and ministry to the Antioch branch of the Orthodox Church in the United
States about ten years before coming to Biola. Five years after his appointment a hyper-Calvinist graduate student launched a crusade against him,
and others on the Biola faculty who had affiliated with his local Orthodox
church community in a nearby city. This crisis exploded into a campus-
wide conflict between factions of students and faculty debating whether or
not the university should hire people who were members or associated with
the Orthodox Church.

Because I had appointed this man to the administrative team, I became
the lightning rod for attack by both students and faculty. As I look back on
this time, my leadership was tested in every way, and in the end, I was not
able to lead the campus nor the factions to reconciliation. The crisis ended
in December of 1998 when the president and the Biola trustees reached an
agreement on how to proceed forward as a Christian University, retaining
the dean and the faculty connected with that local Orthodox church, while

creating a special committee of theology faculty to review church affiliation for all future appointments. The emotional and intellectual intensity of this crisis was so severe that I lost the trust of many in the opposition and we together wounded the dean of students such that his health was broken. I spent hours in anguished prayer during this crisis, and in the end, knew that I had betrayed the dean and failed to lead faculty and students in a manner that built trust within the community and glorified God.

In the year following this crisis, I processed these painful memories with a few colleagues and with my wife. Dallas Willard, friend and former Biola trustee, sent me a copy of his then new book, *The Divine Conspiracy*, which I found a rich resource for reflection on my thinking and actions in the crisis. Looking back in horror, I saw how an unguarded moment of speaking with contempt to two colleagues had unleashed a fire of intense opposition to me and the dean. My judgment and condemnation of people on both sides yielded further grief and rebounded against me, as Jesus warned in Matthew 7:1–5. As I pondered this crisis, my agonized reflection on my use of authority and power as a leader brought me to fresh and transforming spiritual discernment about myself, and my leadership habits and practice.

Flourishing without Suffering: An Illusion

The definitions of "flourish" in *Webster's Unabridged Dictionary* include the following:

1. Originally to blossom

2. To thrive; to grow luxuriantly, to increase and enlarge; (as a tree)

3. To be prosperous, to increase in wealth or honor;

4. To be at the peak of development, activity, influence, etc., to be in one's prime.[1]

Trebesch defines flourishing as "to live within an optimal range of human functioning, when that connotes goodness, generativity, growth, and resilience." In contrast, "languishing" refers to "people who describe their lives as hollow or empty."[2] These definitions reflect a common cultural understanding of Americans about flourishing. A flourishing life and leader is

1. *Webster's New Universal Unabridged Dictionary*, s.v. "flourish."
2. Trebesch, *Made to Flourish*, 179.

defined by thriving in one's social and emotional well-being and enjoying material, social and missional success.

Most leaders and followers imagine successful leadership as vision driven, growth oriented, goal achieving, and leading to personal career advancement. Virtually hundreds of books have been written to guide readers in the essential steps for leaders to advance their careers and achieve such goals. For most people, suffering of any kind is anathema to flourishing. Many believe that suffering is unjust, and without meaning or purpose; many, under the pressures of illness, severe accident, or natural disaster ask, "Where is God, and why does God permit such human tragedies?"

Lee Ellis, in his book *Leading with Honor*, provides a striking contrast to this cultural understanding, telling the stories of men who in the midst of intense physical abuse, emotional persecution, hunger, sickness, and torture as prisoners of war, managed to flourish both individually and in community. Ellis and Andy Crouch share a different understanding of what it means to flourish. As we have seen in chapter 4, for Crouch to flourish is to embrace authority and vulnerability in a way that emulates the life of Jesus Christ; Crouch explains this "paradox of flourishing" as the continuing interchange of "the two dimensions of Jesus' life, his vulnerability in dependence and death on the one hand, his authority in his earthly ministry and his heavenly exaltation on the other."[3]

As I was pondering if and how I might write this book, I was inspired by the symphonic poem of Richard Strauss, "Death and Transfiguration." As I listened repeatedly to this music, I meditated upon the agony of the suffering and death of Jesus, and the triumphant glory of his resurrection, and the miracle of his resurrection body, so changed that his disciples did not recognize this one who had suffered such an agonizing death on the cross. I also contemplated the words of our Lord in John's Gospel, "Unless a kernel of wheat falls to the ground and dies, it remains only a single seed" (John 12:24).

Later, reading Paul's words in 2 Corinthians 4, I have interpreted them as the apostle's narrative poem of death and transfiguration. Paul's poem reminds us that we begin this journey in "jars of clay." As humans, we come from dust and return to dust; as servants of Christ, he is the potter and we are the clay; God makes us for his purpose, and as in the case of Pharaoh, King Saul, and other leaders, he discards some as broken shards when we rebel against him and refuse to do his will. But for those who are willing

---

3. Crouch, *Strong and Weak*, 2–18.

to "fall into the ground and die," the all-surpassing power of God fills and transfigures us into the likeness of Jesus Christ.

Paul describes "falling into the ground" this way:

> We are hard pressed on every side, but not crushed; perplexed, but not in despair; persecuted, but not abandoned; struck down, but not destroyed. We always carry around in our body the death of Jesus, so that the life of Jesus may also be revealed in our body. (2 Cor 4:8–10)

When we submit to the vulnerability of life in Christ, dying to the habits of self-preservation, the life of Jesus is revealed in our bodies, and people see Jesus living in us! By some means we are changed; we look different, we act differently, we lead as shepherds of his flock. Yet, the dying never stops; it is a continuous part of living in Christ. Once again Paul describes it this way: "For we who are alive are always being given over to death for Jesus' sake, so that his life may also be revealed in our mortal body. So then, death is at work in us, but life is at work in you" (2 Cor 4:11–12).

Our transfiguration is through the glory of his life, revealed in us, and the outworking of that life in those to whom God sends us for ministry. Ministry prospers, reaching more and more people with the good news of life in Jesus, so that the church multiplies, and the people respond in an overflow of thanksgiving and praise to the glory of God. It is the blessing of witness, response, and the hope of eternal glory that lifts us beyond the pressures and sacrifice. Once again in Paul's words:

> Therefore we do not lose heart. Though outwardly we are wasting away, yet inwardly we are being renewed day by day. For our light and momentary troubles are achieving for us an eternal glory that far outweighs them all. So we fix our eyes not on what is seen, but on what is unseen, since what is seen is temporary, but what is unseen is eternal. (2 Cor 4:16–18)

How incredibly encouraging are these words! Flourishing comes through both the suffering and vulnerability of our ministry life, and the "all-surpassing power" from God that renews us day by day. So how does this actually work out in daily life and practice of ministry?

Flourishing: The Graces of Vulnerability

The metaphor of "treasure in clay pots" (Common English Bible[4]) suggests a grave contradiction of priorities. Treasure is something so valuable, that in human terms it should be secured by the very best measures, and kept hidden from view. To imagine treasure in clay pots is to imagine either an extremely careless owner, or one so terrifying and powerful that no thief would consider touching those pots. The largest clay pots are fragile, easily broken, and utterly insecure as a place of storage. They are, however, very useful vessels to store and move grain or water for human consumption.

Paul's message in this text is that frail human vessels have been given the responsibility and privilege to carry a great treasure, "the light of the knowledge of God's glory in the face of Jesus Christ" (2 Cor 4:6 CEB). Throughout this book I have examined in various ways the pattern of responses of frail human vessels to leadership crises, and with the help of Andy Crouch we have seen how our attempts to avoid vulnerability lead to exploiting, suffering, and withdrawal. But we have learned that the way of Jesus is to embrace his vulnerability as emphatically as we embrace his power and authority. Paul illustrates this so profoundly, "We always carry around in our body the death of Jesus, so that the life of Jesus may also be revealed in our body" (2 Cor 4:10).

Joshua Kang, in his reflections on the *Spirituality of Gratitude*, reminds us of the graces that we receive when we respond with gratitude to the afflictions we share, while we "carry around in our body the death of Jesus." The first is the "grace of descending." Crouch reminds us that through the cross, Jesus made the ultimate descent from his eternal glory to the suffering and shame of the cross, and then into the grave to the imprisoned spirits (1 Pet 3:19).[5] Kang suggests that "there is an unexplainable depth at the bottom that simply cannot be felt at the top, which is why those used by God's hand all experience serious hardships."[6] At the bottom in my 1998 crisis, I felt utterly challenged and inadequate in my job, my authority, and my knowledge of the community and people with whom I worked. On my knees, face to face with the Spirit and the Scripture, I understood what it meant to die to my old expectations and habits of leadership. It was at the

---

4. Hereafter CEB.

5. Crouch, *Strong and Weak*, 138–39.

6. Kang, *Spirituality of Gratitude*, 18.

bottom that I found the shallowness of my own wisdom, and gratitude for the vastness of the mercy and grace of the Lord Jesus Christ.

The second grace of vulnerability is "isolation." In the agony of public mocking, rejection, insults, and suffering in darkness on the cross, Jesus cried out, "My God, my God, why have you forsaken me?" (Matt 27:46). Such public ridicule and isolation is a frequent experience for leaders in crisis. The risk of rejection and abandonment increases a leader's stress, prompting many to use authority to rectify the situation, which in turn incites greater recrimination by those who refuse to follow. In the middle of my crisis in 1998, I felt completely responsible and utterly alone; my hours of prayer seemed to affect nothing, while the opposition seemed to gain strength and power. Kang reminds us that periods of isolation are often necessary to increase our trust in God, and through gratitude to discover the contentment of "forgiving and blessing those who have isolated us."[7]

I took one step further in processing anew this 1998 crisis in 2008—I retold the story to twenty international church leaders while spending a semester in residency with them at the Overseas Ministry Study Center. It was in this telling of the story that I discovered the third grace of humility.[8] After giving these ministry peers permission to ask me anything about the situation, I answered them as fully as I could remember. Then I asked them to teach me: What false assumptions did I make? What opportunities did I miss? After an hour of conversation together about my story, and then an hour of reflection in four small groups, they astonished me with their love, their insights, and suggestions. My initial reaction was—where were you all when I needed you in 1998? My second reaction was of deep gratitude for the grace of God extended through them to me when I humbled myself to share this painful story. Paul reminds us that we are to "have the same mindset as Christ Jesus: who . . . humbled himself by becoming obedient to death—even death on a cross" (Phil 2:5–8).

The fourth grace of vulnerability is brokenness,[9] shattered by pain, sorrow, scars, and despair from the long siege of crisis. Mark (15:15–20) reminds us that Jesus was flogged, crowned with thorns, struck on the head with a staff, and mocked and spit upon by soldiers before they led him away to be crucified. Jesus gave his body and blood as an offering for our redemption. Brokenness is an offering to God, one that God multiplies in

7. Ibid., 20.

8. Ibid., 22–23.

9. Ibid., 24–25.

blessing, just as Jesus broke five loaves to feed the five thousand. When I shared the story of my brokenness to my brothers and sisters in Christ at OMSC in 2008, I discovered how desperately a leader needs counsel from other trustworthy members of the body of Christ. They taught me the power and love of the body of Christ, and the rich resources that are available to a leader who will take the risk of inviting them into a crisis, and seeking their wisdom about pathways forward. Crisis and brokenness are astonishing opportunities for learning and change; when we share the risks and challenges with others, and trust God to lead, our authority is enhanced and our capacity to embrace meaningful risk in faith is strengthened. We are in the best possible position to flourish.

Flourishing: To Fix Our Eyes on What Is Unseen

The foundation for change for leaders, teams, and congregations is to refocus our lives upon our covenant relationship with God, which begins by centering our thoughts and worship on our new identity in Christ. Our initial act of faith in Jesus Christ brings us into a new covenant relationship with Jesus, granted to us through his blood for the forgiveness of our sins. But more importantly, that covenant relationship includes the call to follow Jesus. We are no longer our own, but rather we are participants with Christ in his body for the work of the kingdom of God. The triune God has made this covenant with us so that our hope and lives may become complete in the fullness of Christ. The word of the Lord in John's gospel makes this so profoundly clear. If we stay connected to him, then he will work in us and through us to accomplish all that he desires. The challenge for us is staying connected.

The pattern of evidence from our one hundred twenty-nine cases shows that every leadership crisis has at its root a temporary disconnect in our relationship with Christ. We somehow become consumed with the issue before us. We become anxious about our relationships with people, and about the outcomes of the activity or goal for which we are working. Instead of trusting God, we take matters into our own hands, and depend upon our own strength and skills to achieve the ends that we believe are right. We lose focus on the goal to bring glory to God, and we seek to make things come out in such a way that we are secure and that our objectives are met. The only way to stop this is to put God in the rightful place in our lives as Lord and Savior. He is the only one who can deliver us from this trap.

Once we understand clearly who we are in Christ, and intentionally discipline ourselves to stay connected with him, we have through him the spiritual will and resources to work on our covenant relationship with others. In the power of the Spirit, we may then exercise our will to listen to and communicate in love with those around us. Through the practice of fellowship and forgiveness, we may build mutual trust and strengthen capacities to work in unity in our communities of faith. When our unity and momentum together is broken in moments of crisis, we may have unwavering confidence in God's commitment to us, and we may focus our efforts as one body, with one spirit and one hope to guide us through the darkness.

Flourishing: The Healing Power of Light

When we intentionally face our crisis, and reflect upon the self that led us to that place, the Lord graciously shines his light into our motives and actions, and begins a process of healing our brokenness. As I have illustrated for you in this book, I personally have found it exceedingly helpful to examine my thinking, values, motives, and action in a particular crisis in my past. By probing deeply into my blindness, false assumptions, and need for vindication, the Holy Spirit has shown me the cracks and weaknesses in my "clay pot." As a frail human being, this kind of reflection has driven me to my knees, as I see more clearly my limitations, my tendency to self-vindication, and how I have been quick to place blame on others who have failed to comply or cooperate with me.

But the good news is that when I have faced my crisis, and have defined and declared how these personal challenges have become habitual in my leadership, God has led me to confession, repentance, and openness to the power of the Holy Spirit to change these patterns in my life. Most of the other leaders who have taken this journey with me have also discovered that God in his power begins a work within us that leads to a deeper relationship with him, and empowers us in the small daily steps that lead to change.

The knowledge that God has chosen us, and has committed to a covenant relationship with us that he will not break, is deeply comforting. In spite of our anxieties and fear of crisis, the Scriptures and our experience assures us that God will not abandon us. We are chosen, holy, and dearly loved (Col 3:12). So then, when we have identified the areas of our blindness, we are eager to work with the Lord Jesus Christ and with others to bring about change.

That work is as simple and as complex as putting on our clothes! The best analogy I can think of is a morning workout. My wife and I begin our day with a cup of coffee, Scripture reading, reflection, prayer, and a two-mile walk together. Following that walk, we enjoy the refreshing experience of a hot shower—water and shampoo that washes away the oils of sleep and the sweat of exercise. After the shower, we dry, blow dry hair, and select our clothing for the day. The clothing can be the most complicated work of the routine, since we have more than we need, providing us with many choices. But the end result is the same—once we are dressed, we look into the mirror, make sure everything looks as we wish, and we are ready to begin our day.

Of all the elements in this morning routine, the Scripture, reflection and prayer phase, and the "mirror" experience are the most important. The Scripture phase is the time in which we reflect upon who we are in Christ, upon the magnitude of the gifts and blessings that have been given to us, and upon the critical needs of the world around us. The sum effect of this experience is to focus anew on our calling in Christ, and upon God's purpose for us as we begin this new day.

The mirror phase is the time when we check to see if we are dressed and ready for whatever comes throughout the day. If we have been paying attention in the Scripture phase, the look in the mirror prompts us to look not only at our hair, face, and clothing, but also to ask, "What is seen, and what is unseen?" For me that is the moment when I ask these questions: Have I clothed myself with compassion, kindness, humility, gentleness, and patience? Am I willing and ready to bear with others, and to forgive whatever grievances that may arise in this day? Have I put on love, which binds these all together in perfect unity? Is the peace of Christ ruling in my heart? And, am I thankful? By the simple act of looking the mirror, I ask again for the Spirit to clothe me for this day in those unseen virtues, and when I do this, he always grants my request.

Now I must confess that I have often found it more difficult to stay dressed with these unseen virtues than I had hoped. After eight years of periodic reflection and dialogue with others to let go some of those old habits, and allow the Holy Spirit to guide and direct my life, there are occasions when I suffer relapse. I have concluded that in my own strength I am trapped in this clay pot, but by the mysterious power of memorized word, and the empowering presence of the Holy Spirit, Christ is at work in me, and he does enable me daily to be more like him. The most challenging times are moments or days of crisis—in those circumstances, I need the support of Judy, and others in the body of Christ around us, to keep my unseen clothing on, and to remember that in Christ we may be "hard pressed on every side, but not crushed; perplexed, but not in despair; persecuted, but not abandoned; struck down, but not destroyed" (2 Cor 4:8).

The Hope of "Transfiguration"—Treasure in Clay Pots

As I have shared with you the stories of my leadership, the Chad story captures the best and the worst of my leadership. I rejoice in the beautiful transforming body work of the international church that participated in this ministry. I weep at the missed opportunities to make disciples at home and to listen, and to speak words of loving kindness in the power of the Holy Spirit to the pastors in Chad. I find that I'm engaged in a continuous process of reflection, reality check with reference to my leadership habits, and then renewal of my relationship in Christ and surrender of my habits to him and to his will. This process for me is best understood as temporary, a partial transfiguration on my journey to be transformed into the likeness of Christ. The reality is that I'm still living and leading in this human clay pot.

Although I have retired from senior leadership positions, I am still active as an elder in my local church. I am also actively mentoring students and leaders. In all of these activities, it is a daily discipline to keep centered on Christ, and not on my previous habits and skills. Every day when I awaken from sleep, my default settings return, but then I look in the mirror for that which is "unseen."

Indeed, there is hope and joy! We have within us the treasure of "the light of the knowledge of God's glory in the face of Jesus Christ" (2 Cor 4:6 CEB). That treasure is an "all-surpassing power," ever present within us for the works that Jesus has called us to do in his will and by his name. I have seen in the writings of the men and women, church and mission leaders, who have partnered with me in facing our leadership crises—they too have discovered this power, and their own ways of centering their lives in Christ.

One friend Berj, struggling with his default habit to fix things in his own power, decided that he needed something visual to remind him daily that the ministry is not his, but God's. Toward that end he placed an empty chair on the opposite side of his desk, and an open Bible on the desk in front of the chair. Each morning as he enters his church office, the empty chair and the open Bible remind him that God is present, and the ministry of that day belongs to God. However, this was not enough to prevent him from default. In the context of meetings and other leadership work, he found the old habits to use his "authority to fix" back in full force. So now in his elder board meetings, he places an empty chair and an open Bible at the front or center of the meeting, and he has shared with his elders that this chair is to remind them all that the agenda is the Lord's. When we begin with the right focus, it is much easier to be faithful and thus glorify God.

I invite you, the reader, to begin your own journey of reflection. Your leadership crises have within them an incredible fund of knowledge about who you are and how you lead in your flesh, which is a clay pot filled with an incredible treasure. If you will partner with the Lord to examine your own stories, the Holy Spirit will guide you into his glorious light, and you will experience his transfiguration of your leadership by filling it with "the light of the knowledge of God's glory in the face of Jesus Christ" (2 Cor 4:6 CEB).

Part Four

GOING FURTHER?

14

Reflection: Your Own Crucible of Crisis

> Everybody knows you can learn a lot by failing. But few people actually know how to do that. . . . Failure is a strategic resource. Like the people you employ, the money you spend or the facilities and technologies you use, it has unique intrinsic value if you're open and wise enough to manage it as such. Treat it like unrefined ore that needs to be processed and examined to reveal its riches. Failure is reality's way of showing you what you don't yet know, but need to learn. It contains the seeds of precisely the insight you've been looking for, if you have the honesty and humility to explore those secrets.
>
> After all, you've already paid its tuition. You might as well get the education that goes with it . . . and stop flunking failure.[1]

The Opportunity for Learning

As I shared at the beginning of this book, reflection on one's leadership crisis may become a powerful tool for learning how to be a more effective leader. Ronald Heifetz has developed what he terms "case-in-point" learning, in which students experience transformative insight and understanding through peer processing of their personal leadership crises. In a five-year study of Heifetz's course at Harvard, Parks documents how case-in-point

1. Danner and Coppersmith, "How Not to Flunk," R2.

teaching seeks to bring action and reflection together in the most immediate way possible for each person.[2] Other scholars have confirmed the power of such learning beyond educational classrooms.[3] My wife, Judy, and I have documented the very significant transformations of pastors and mission leaders using this method in our doctor of ministry classes.

As a reader of this book, you probably will not have an opportunity to take a class on this subject, but this opportunity for learning is as available to you in your present ministry context, as it would be to someone who enrolls in a class. You can do this alone, or if you are the most senior leader, you might employ this process as a tool for mentoring and growth within your leadership team. The price of such learning for each person is taking the time to spend a day with God, and begin the process of reflection, as I will outline below. That day with God is certainly the most important step you can take toward learning from your crises. The Holy Spirit is ever present with us, and is waiting for us to invite the Spirit, and be willing to listen to what the Spirit has to say about our crises. But that alone is not enough; "case-in-point" learning begins with the discipline of writing the story of your crisis situation in leadership that did not proceed as you intended, and did not achieve the results you sought.

A Day of Reflection

If you are willing to take the risk, the first step in this journey is to ask the Holy Spirit to guide you in a day of reflection on your past ministry. You might begin that reflection with a time of gratitude and thanksgiving, looking back over your leadership journey, and celebrating God's goodness in every way you can remember. This is essential to the whole process, since through faith you have died to your old self and been raised with Christ, and called into his service; you have indeed experienced the glory and blessing of that special relationship and place with him. This is also a moment to humble yourself, and acknowledge to God that these moments of pleasure and rejoicing were God's gift to you, as God multiplied your small offerings and did a greater work than you could have done yourself.

In your second session of prayer, I suggest that you take a walk, and during that walk, ask the Holy Spirit to lead you once again through the difficult times. Allow the Holy Spirit to guide this journey, bringing to your

2. See Parks, *Leadership Can Be Taught*, 6–11.

3. See Armstrong, *Learning*; Danner and Coppersmith, *Other "F" Word*.

mind those moments when you were suffering, when your expectations were not met, and when your leadership ended in places where you would not have gone, if you could have seen the end of that journey. Keep on walking, keep on praying, and let the Holy Spirit speak to you about that and other events in your leadership that did not go well. As you listen to the Holy Spirit, you will discern the moment of crisis that God wants you to process further.

Once you have discerned the specific crisis that troubles your spirit, the next step is to allow the Holy Spirit to guide you into deeper reflection on those crisis moments and your leadership thoughts and behaviors. At this point, it is good to sit down in a quiet place and make notes on your cell phone or a piece of paper you have brought for this purpose. Again, trust the Holy Spirit to guide you. For some the story will appear like a collage of photos engaging people, places, meetings, emotions, and disappointments; for others, the story may be a timeline of events with a beginning, middle, and end; and for still others, the story may surface memories of critical conversations or heated exchanges between people important to the crisis and to your leadership. It is important to write down enough about these memories that you may return to reflect upon them at a later time.

At this point, you are likely feeling emotional, spiritual, and physical fatigue. This is the time to find rest and peace in the Spirit. If you have emotions of pain and regret, take these to the Lord for confession and healing. You may wish to sing or listen to worship songs by others. You may go to lunch, or spend time in silence, focusing on God's mercy and grace in your life. Physical exercise is good—walking, running, biking, swimming, or some other activity that frees your mind and emotions from the pain of your reflection on the crisis moment.

Writing Your Case-in-Point

After you have put some distance from the deep emotional time of self-reflection, the most important work of the day begins—writing the story in such a way that you may share it with others. The purpose of writing is not to write down everything that happened, but instead to highlight those critical moments of your leadership in the story, revealed to you in your earlier time with God (see table 14.1). The purpose of this work is to narrow your reflection in such a way that you reveal your emotions and values, and provide details of the crisis moments when you used your authority and power, made a decision, or acted to influence or direct others toward your desired outcome. Finally, review and write what you feel were the consequences of your actions or decisions.

TABLE 14.1 Questions for Reflection and Writing a Case Study of Crisis	
Crisis Moments	What were the crisis moments? Who were the others, and how did they take sides in the conflict?
Emotions & Values	What emotions did you and the others experience during the crisis? What were the belief and value conflicts that are evident in the case?
Authority & Power	When and how did you use your authority and power—control of systems/resources/relationships—to achieve some desired outcome?
Actions	How did you work to manage the persons/interest groups involved? Describe the decisions and action that you took to address the issues.
Outcomes	What were the outcomes of your leadership in this crisis?

In your crisis story it is important to name the people who played significant roles in that crisis, and to reflect how each one contributed to your thinking and actions. It is also helpful to note if they shared your values or had conflicting values and behaviors. If possible, comment about the distress you all felt in that situation, and how you sought to manage that distress. Limit yourself to about 1500 words, so that you can share this with others, and invite them to reflect on this story with you.

Opening Oneself to the Light: Trusted Peers

After you have completed writing your personal narrative of a leadership crisis, the next step is to invite three or four trusted peers to process this story with you. These people should not be individuals that report to you, or that see you in an authority relationship to them. If you are a senior pastor, you might invite some fellow senior pastors in your city to serve you in this way. You could mix up the group by asking a couple of pastors to come and invite one of their associates or elders to join them. It is best to have people, men and women, that you respect highly in this peer group. They need not be close friends, but rather people who share your passion for the church, and that you believe are open to the Holy Spirit, and willing to seek with you the presence of God in this process.

The invitation should be clear—you are asking them to first prayerfully read your story, and then to help you answer two questions: what false assumptions did I make in this crisis, and what opportunities did I miss? However, it is important to coach them to defer answers to these questions until after they have sat with you and the others, and processed the story together with you, asking both clarifying questions and probing in the presence of the Holy Spirit deeper issues that may have led you to false assumptions and missed opportunities.

You may ask one of these people to prayerfully lead this process, as your spiritual advocate (see table 14.2). Or you may ask the group to select the person they believe would serve you all well. Since you are presenting your case, you need to empower another to facilitate the process, and help members keep focus on the purpose—listening carefully to you, probing together what you were feeling, thinking, and doing in that crisis, and exposing the termites of self that drove your emotions, thoughts, and actions. If the group somehow gets sidetracked on trying to give you advice on how to fix the problem, they and you will completely miss the point. The goal is to expose the "termites of self" that led you down that path to crisis, not to find some technical way to fix an old problem.

TABLE 14.2 The Role of Spiritual Advocate	
Prayer	Inviting the Presence of the Holy Spirit, Ears to Hear, Eyes to See
Case Presentation (30 minutes)	Invite you to share an overview of your written story of crisis. Invite follow-up questions by participants and your response.
Case Clarification (30 minutes)	Invite questions for "clarification" of the written and oral story; Assure that all participants have an opportunity to ask.
Refining Fire (50 minutes?)	Invite "exposing termite" questions—hungers, values, default habits? Invite questions about feelings, judging, wants/needs?
Discernment (20 minutes?)	Facilitate dialogue re: false assumptions and missed opportunities, and About hungers, values, default habits at the root of these issues

Toward this end, the spiritual advocate will guide the members to listen first to you, and ask you questions that allow you to clarify for them what you were feeling, thinking, and valuing in this situation. The group may explore with you how you responded to others in the crisis, and how you used your authority and power to achieve your goals. In this short time of discussion, it is not necessary or helpful to surface all of the details, but more importantly to surface and to understand your thinking, emotions, and actions in the crisis.

So, as the case presenter of your leadership crisis, your opportunity is to ask these brothers and sisters in Christ to help you discern more clearly the default habits, hungers, values, thinking, and emotions that surfaced in this crisis. You need not and should not look for a solution to a problem, even if the issue is ongoing; rather the better way is to open your heart, to fall willingly in humility before the Spirit of God, and to ask God to deliver you from anything that may keep you from dying to self, and following Jesus through this or a new difficult challenge.

If you are willing to ask your friends to do this work, then you must in humility empower them to ask you deep, refining fire questions that disclose issues of heart and mind. You must give them permission to probe into the thoughts, feelings, expectations, and emotional and spiritual needs that occupied you during the crisis. And then, prayerfully ask the Holy Spirit to enable you to respond in openness and humility to them, trusting that in the power of the Holy Spirit, they will love you and lead you to the discernment you need to grow and change (see table 14.3).

TABLE 14.3 "Refining Fire" Questions to Expose "Termites of Self" to Light	
What was I thinking?	False assumptions? Incorrect diagnosis? Poor data? Default reasoning?
What was I feeling about risk, loss, public response?	Anger? Fear? Hope? Optimism? Opportunity? Frustration?
How was I blinded?	My experience? Expectations? Values? Assessment of others?
What did I want/need emotionally, spiritually?	Relief? Sympathy? Control? Assurance? Significance? Recognition?
How did I judge others and myself?	Rigid, incompetent, aggressive, undermining, ignorant?
What did I miss that might be helpful?	People, opportunities, values, allies?

If you or they focus on "what to do" questions (What did I do wrong? What could I do to fix it?—see table 14.4), you will once again go down the pathway of blaming others and seeking technical solutions to complex problems that end in leadership crisis. It is critical that they ask and you respond to the deeper questions that lead you to self-discovery and self-disclosure.

TABLE 14.4 Unproductive Questions for Processing Crises	
"Do wrong" questions	What did I do wrong?
	What did they do wrong?
	Whose fault was it?
"Fix it" questions	What could I do better?
	What if I did this? Or that?
	How can I solve this problem?

Judy and I have used the metaphor of the "wok," a large stir-fry pan, to characterize the peer reflection on leadership cases of crisis. When the members of the group are filled with the Holy Spirit, and they work together to "stir-fry" the details given to them by the case presenter, the heat of the process and the light of the Holy Spirit become a refining fire exposing "termites of self" that threaten, undermine and even destroy the presence and power of the word and the Spirit of God in our inner being.

It is essential for both the case presenter and the trusted peers to reject the "what to do" questions, and focus together on the questions that force the "termites of self" into the light. This work takes prayer, practice on the part of the participants, and the careful oversight of the spiritual advocate to be sure that the participants are not distracted by our cultural need to "fix" a problem, and ignore God's work to reconcile his people to himself.

Will to Embrace the Light?

The outcome of such a case-in-point process is, in large part, dependent upon you, the case presenter. You have taken the first step of disclosing your crisis in writing. You have then taken the second step to submit yourself to the Holy Spirit, and the probing of a company of trusted friends, with the purpose of going deeper, and asking God to expose any "termites of self" to the light of his word and the Spirit. During that process you chose to reveal, or not, areas of hunger and brokenness in your life, and to allow these friends to minister to you in these areas. At the end of this process, you know where you are in your relationship to God and to the others.

Change is very difficult, and we most often resist change because of a fear of loss, rather than a fear of what we might become. Jesus invites us to die to self, and in so doing, to enter into a life in him that does indeed carry a cross, but at the same time is full of the joy of our Lord. Therefore, the challenge for each case presenter is to accept this invitation. Are we willing to listen to the Spirit, to allow the light of Christ and the refining fire of his word to purify our hearts and minds? If so, then there is more work to do.

We cannot learn new behaviors in one two-hour meeting with friends. This kind of reflection is critical, and allows us to name the "termites of self" that have power to destroy us. Naming the "termites" is the beginning of dying to self, and refocusing on Christ. But, unless we are willing to act on the discernment that comes from light, and respond in a positive way to break old habits, replace old hungers, and grow in faith, it will come to nothing. Kevin Ford describes these issues as "red zone" problems, that when left unattended, destroy any effort at effective leadership.[4]

We must concede that God's glory and God's people have higher priority than our old leadership goals and agendas. And we must begin the spiritual work of submitting our leadership strengths and habits to Christ, and inviting God and God's people to help us be transfigured into the image of Christ.

In the following chapter, I will share how God has been working in many of our leadership peers to do the hard work of practice, so that you may "stand firm. Let nothing move you. Always give yourselves fully to the work of the Lord, because you know that your labor in the Lord is not in vain" (1 Cor 15:58).

---

4. Ford, *Transforming Church*, 114.

15

Remembering the Past, Rehearsing a Future

We asked at the beginning of part 2 of this book, "What does it mean to die to self and refocus our leadership around who we are in Christ?" We have learned that our culture, hungers, and habits of life predispose us to depend upon our strengths to lead in ministry. Such leading is a form of idolatry—"I know what to do, and let's get on with it"—instead of, "God knows what I should do, Lord help me to listen and obey." Our reflections on stories of crisis have confirmed that self-reliance in all of its forms undermines our relationship with Christ, and thus our leadership effectiveness. Further, while we may actually succeed in our goal, as I described in the previous chapter, we fail to achieve God's purpose in our ministries.

This final chapter is about leaders who have gathered to remember the past, to repent of their self-assurance, of their self-centered and sometimes hunger-driven leadership, and to renew their commitment to, and connection with our Lord Jesus Christ. We acknowledge that we are the people of the new covenant, made through his blood, shed for the forgiveness of our sins, and we have been baptized into a community of faith dedicated to spreading the gospel and making disciples of all who will follow Jesus. We have prayerfully faced our crises, and have examined our hearts to uncover pride, arrogance, fear, hungers, self-focus, and resistance to the Spirit in our lives and leadership. We have humbled ourselves before the Lord, and have listened to the words of Jesus, "Unless a kernel of wheat falls into the ground and dies, it remains only a single seed . . . whoever serves me must follow me" (John 12:23). The purpose of this chapter is to guide the reader to imagine and rehearse a future that is different from the past. By looking back, and understanding what we have done, we now intentionally reframe that one past crisis as a rehearsal of our desired future in obedience to Christ.

This chapter describes two specific spiritual practices of reflection on a specific crisis and rehearsal of change. The first is to write a script and then role play certain critical moments in one's case study of leadership crisis, engaging with friends who have helped us process our case study. The written script, role play, and conversation after is a deliberate act of talking to each other in the presence of the Lord about the things we had done that were displeasing to God, and then rehearsing together how we might, instead, honor the Lord, given those same circumstances. Our desire is to make an offering to God of not only our repentance, but also to die to these old ways, and more specifically, practice right action that would be pleasing to him in that same situation.

The second spiritual practice is to write a "scroll of remembrance," reflecting both on the past and the future, remembering what the Holy Spirit has taught us throughout this process, and asking God to guide us to steps of renewal in our relationship with God and our relationships with others. In this concluding chapter I will describe further these two practices and share some of the stories of those who have done them.

Deeper Reflection—a Default Role Play

Brent, senior pastor of a large church on the east coast, writes: "The Role Play Simulation Exercises were shockingly revealing to me. I learned things most powerfully when writing out in role play, my ministry crisis. This learning process took me totally off guard and proved to be perhaps the most powerful learning experience of my week." As Brent testifies so passionately, the reframing of your case study into a role play of conversations and actions moves you to a much deeper level of understanding. When you actually try to write down the things you have said, and remember how others have responded, you begin to see the story in new light. The new light comes because, through your earlier conversations about your case, the Holy Spirit has opened your eyes and removed much of the blindness of self-confidence and perhaps self-justification about it.

Writing a "default role play" begins with the text of your case study of crisis. In that story, you have already set forth the key outline of the crisis and in your peer group reflection you have hopefully uncovered much of what you were thinking, how you were feeling, and some of the old habits, fears, values, and even personal hungers that your enemy, the devil, uses to undermine you in times of crisis. To write the role play, you need to select two or three critical moments in your story (see table 15.1) and replay those moments in your mind and on paper. Reconstructing parts of those conversations is essential to this exercise, remembering your responses to what you believe the others said. As you reconstruct each, the Holy Spirit will reveal to you the assumptions (true or false) that you made, the words that you used that hurt or encouraged others, and the dialogue that led you all deeper down the path of your leadership crisis.

When you have finished writing these conversations, take time to prayerfully look again at you own words and actions, and ask the Holy Spirit to help you see clearly which words and actions were not the offering you wanted to give to God and to his people. At this point you are ready to write the two summaries. The first is to articulate anew those areas of your leadership that you want to surrender to Christ, the "default summary" of values, habits, fears, and hungers that the enemy will use to destroy you. The second is to count the cost; what was the outcome of these conversations and what did this cost you and the others entrusted to you by the Lord Jesus Christ.

TABLE 15.1 Writing the "Default" Role Play	
Critical Moments:	What were the two or three critical moments in your story where you took the wrong path?
Conversations:	To whom did you speak in each of those critical moments? What did you say? What did each of the others say?
Script Dialogue:	Reconstruct your conversations in script or outline form that others can role play with you.
Default Summary:	Summarize what you now see in your conversations and actions as default values, habits, fears, and personal hungers evident to you.
Outcomes:	What happened? And what was the cost to all involved?

As you allow God's light to shine into the darkness of this leadership crisis, the Holy Spirit will show you more clearly the other people, their motives, and the causes and consequences of your actions. Joel reports:

> Writing the role play made me feel closer to the other people involved in my case. As I tried to "get inside their heads" it built some empathy in me for each of them. It helped me value how they perceive things that are different from me. In some sense, it helped me listen to them better and process why they acted the way they did and what they may have valued that was different from me.
>
> Acting out the role play engaged me at the emotional level regarding my default pattern. I found myself getting teary at times during the role play and I did not anticipate that. Role playing brought me close to some of my feeling of sadness and grief about how my default precipitated pain in the life of my church family and the elder team.

Joel's deeper understanding of the others through writing the role play is a gift from God; once he has gained that understanding, he is already a better servant to them, and to others. To appreciate and value the other members of the body, especially in situations of crisis, is the beginning of love, and that is what we so often fail to do. The writing also forces us to remember what we have heard in the past, and to listen more carefully in the future.

Joel also notes that the actual performance of the role play has an even more powerful impact for us. The writing is an intellectual task, requiring both memory and organization of information, but the experience of acting out the role play is emotional. Even with our partly scripted conversations, and the stilted responses from our helpers, we feel both the emotion of our first experience, and the grief that Joel shares about how our words and actions created pain for others. You gain the most from a role play when you actually perform it with friends, and have a conversation together before the Lord when you are finished. God speaks in the power of his Spirit to our minds and our hearts through the role play process, and in the conversation after, as we allow him to enter these secret places.

Once we see clearly our old habits, the Spirit challenges us to let go, to stop trying to control people and events, and to trust God that when we obey him, the burden of responsibility now belongs to God, and we truly become God's servants. But for many of us, controlling people and process is so deeply embedded in our life experience, letting go requires deep commitment and practice. Jeff notes:

To release control to this extent will take a profound work of God's Spirit in my life. But, as I mentioned, this is exactly what I am praying for and seeking. After the role play exercise in class, . . . [and] processing what I learned in the simulation, I wrote, "I really need people. I need people to help me jointly process and make decisions, not just to endorse decisions I have already unilaterally made. I need people with whom to mutually interact in meaningful ways, not just to control as I seek to accomplish tasks. I need people I can be 'responsible to,' not to rescue or save."

Defining New Direction—a Covenant-with-God Replay

When God speaks to us, these new insights are painful on one hand, but also may be full of hope. A Covenant-with-God replay provides the opportunity to look ahead, and ask the questions, what could I have done differently in this situation, and how may I allow the Holy Spirit to lead me into leadership that is transfigured into a reflection of the Lord Jesus Christ? As we consciously reflect on what it means to be part of the body of Christ, and on God's words for us as to how we might live as his chosen people (1 Pet 2:12–16), holy and dearly loved (Col 3:12), the Spirit reveals to us new pathways to more effective leadership. By thinking through our default conversations and reframing them around our commitment to obey our Lord Jesus, we discover ways of obedience that were not evident to us before.

The Covenant-with-God replay begins with some new assumptions. First, I am in a new covenant relationship with God through the blood of Jesus Christ, and in that relationship, I have been given the glory of God in order that we together may reflect that glory to others (John 17:22–23); second, in that relationship I have been called and entrusted by the Lord Jesus himself to make disciples and to shepherd his flock; third, I understand that to follow Jesus is to obey his first command, to love one another as he has loved us. Once we have understood that our calling is not about the worship service, the programs, the buildings, staffing, and operations of a church or mission, we are ready to ask a simple question: If I could go back in time and rethink and replay my leadership, focused first on giving glory to God, and then to love and disciple those men and women that God had entrusted to me, what would I do differently?

The actual writing of this role play begins with your default role play (see table 15.2). The task, given your new assumptions, is to rethink and rewrite your words, conversations and actions, asking what would be pleasing to God in each critical moment. However, you can only change *your* words and actions! You cannot assume that anyone else will change. However, you may guess how others might respond to your new words. You must also be realistic, your fears or emotions may be the same, so the risk of "letting go" may test your faith in God even more than before! As you seek direction from the Holy Spirit, the Spirit will guide you to reframe your leadership. You will learn from God's word, you will learn from what you read here, and you will learn from the testimonies of others who, in Christ, have accepted this same challenge.[1]

TABLE 15.2 Writing the "Covenant-with-God" Role Play	
Critical Moments:	In the same critical moments of the "default" role play, what new assumptions will you make about your purpose and role?
Conversations:	Rethink each of the conversations in your "default" role play. What do you wish you had said in these conversations?
Script Dialogue:	Rescript your default conversations—writing new versions for yourself—assuming that the others may not change.
Covenant-with-God Summary:	Summarize new options that you intend to cultivate in Christ; Spiritual work (word, prayer), Body work (listening, love), Leading: releasing control, empowering others, etc.
Outcomes:	What hopes? Cost/benefit of following Jesus?

As with the default role play, the actual performance has an even more powerful impact than the writing. Chuck testifies:

> When I played the covenant-with-God replay it was like a healing balm to this failure. It is one thing to know I exercise leadership in a wrong way, it is another to actually articulate the better way. I was forced to answer the question, what would the Holy Spirit want me to do to maintain my integrity before God as well as honoring the community of faith in covenant-with-God relationships.

---

1. For examples of Default and Covenant Role Play scripts, see Lingenfelter, *Re-Visioning*, 11–20.

Through the covenant-with-God role play, the Holy Spirit jars us with the reality of our habits, and points us back to our relationship with Christ, and building unity in his body, the disciples that he has given to us.

One of the most important benefits of actually doing the role play comes in the emotional healing that God gives to leaders. Failure is always painful, and the pain of some failures stay with us for years after the crisis has passed. Some carry the pain into new ministries, and though it lies hidden beneath the surface, it clings like a virus to our spiritual being, and strikes again in new situations of stress. Emotional healing comes when we submit the fault and pain to the healing touch of Jesus. Wayne, a district superintendent, writes:

> Addressing my default, especially illustrated in the second role play showed me the value of team, and of learning to distinguish "self" from "role." . . . Dead to self, I am empowered by the Spirit to graciously address situations, which I failed to address in my case study of failure. The discussions of all the case studies reminded me afresh of the value of power giving leadership. Ministry failure is so often traced back to a clenching fist, and a tight knot, which speaks of my need to control. Life giving ministry comes from release and giving away what I cannot keep.

As Wayne so powerfully testifies, by actually doing the covenant-with-God role play in a small community of our peers, God does a remarkable work within us and among us. In dying to self, we experience within our soul the presence and grace of the Holy Spirit that in turn fills us with grace and strength to empower others. Among us, the Spirit touches all who have been with us in our journey, radiating the glory of Christ in such a way that we all are changed.

Rehearsing a Possible Future

The prophet Malachi, on an occasion when the priests and Levites who feared the Lord had gathered and talked to one another, records that "the LORD listened and heard. A scroll of remembrance was written in his presence concerning those who feared the LORD and honored his name" (3:16). I can only presume that their conversation was about the words of the prophet, and their collective collapse as the spiritual leaders of Israel. The conversation was clearly a turn of direction for them, renewing their fear and reverence for the Lord, and recommitting themselves to be men of God, and living and leading in such a way that God would be glorified among the people of Israel and the nations. And the text reports that God listened, and was pleased, so much so that God called for a scroll of remembrance to be written in his presence, testifying of this event in which these men revered and honored his name.

I have asked many men and women—those who have taken this journey of reflecting deeply on their leadership crisis—to write their own scrolls of remembrance, testifying to God's work in their life and leadership. As you have read in the quotes above, many have openly confessed how they had lost their way as leaders. Humbly before brothers and sisters in Christ, they have confessed how their failures are rooted in a loss of focus on the glory of Christ, and upon his primary call as disciples to stay connected to him. Further they have lost sight of his primary mission to make disciples, and to be one together in the glory of his death, resurrection, and love. Each has written a testimony of commitment and *will* to first, die to their old habits as leaders, and second, to the work of obedience that leads to transformation through the power of the Spirit into faithful followers of the Lord Jesus Christ.

The beauty of our experience is that we together have taken this journey in the presence of the Holy Spirit. We know that it was not the case-in-point method, it was not the writing of our stories, it was not the peer review of those stories, and it was not writing and performing role plays. All of these things were just means by which we sought to examine ourselves, to repent of our sins, and to ask and listen to the Holy Spirit about next steps. Our goal from the beginning was to renew and strengthen our relationship and daily walk with Jesus, and to submit afresh to his will and to the work of his Spirit in our hearts, lives and leadership. As I have read the many "scrolls" written by these men and women, I believe that God has written his own scroll of remembrance in their hearts. I conclude this book with the testimony of Dave about God's work in his life and leadership:

> To change my default patterns of leadership, I realize that I must "stay in the river"—walk closely with God and be empowered by the Holy Spirit. When I am living this way, I see more clearly the realities around me and also live more by faith in what God can do instead of fear of what man might do. Having a "covenant with God" focus means that I allow Him to lead me, slowing me down to discern his voice and keeping me aware what He desires to do in the lives of those around me. The Lord showed me . . . that, on my own, I will continue to revert to my insecurities and default

patterns. Leading as a partner with God, however, is a reality because "with God all things are possible." This reminder greatly encouraged me to seek him always for the power to lead as Christ would lead.

References

Armstrong, Terry. "Learning from Failures in O.D. Consulting." *Organization Development Journal* 27 (2009) 71–77.

Bolman, Lee G., and Terrence E. Deal. *Modern Approaches to Understanding and Managing Organizations*. San Francisco: Jossey-Bass, 1984.

Crouch, Andy. *Strong and Weak: Embracing a Life of Love, Risk, and True Flourishing*. Downers Grove: InterVarsity, 2016.

Danner, John, and Mark Coppersmith. "How Not to Flunk at Failure." *Wall Street Journal*, October 26, 2015.

———. *The Other "F" Word: How Smart Leaders, Teams, and Entrepreneurs Put Failure to Work*. New York: Wiley, 2015.

Ellis, Lee. *Leading with Honor: Leadership Lessons from the Hanoi Hilton*. FreedomStar Media, 2012.

Ford, Kevin G. *Transforming Church: Bringing Out the Good to Get to Great*. Carol Stream, IL: SaltRiver, 2007.

Gupta, Paul R., and Sherwood Lingenfelter. *Breaking Tradition to Accomplish Vision: Training Leaders for a Church-Planting Movement*. Winona Lake, IN: BMH, 2006.

Heifetz, Ronald A. *Leadership without Easy Answers*. Cambridge: Belknap of Harvard University Press, 1994.

Heifetz, Ronald A., et al. *The Practice of Adaptive Leadership*. Boston: Harvard Business, 2009.

Heifetz, Ronald A., and Marty Linsky. *Leadership on the Line: Staying Alive through the Dangers of Leading*. Boston: Harvard Business, 2002.

Hofstede, Geert H., et al. *Cultures and Organizations: Software of the Mind*. 3rd ed. New York: McGraw-Hill, 2010.

Kang, Joshua Choonmin. *Spirituality of Gratitude: The Unexpected Blessings of Thankfulness*. Downers Grove: InterVarsity, 2015.

Kennedy, Lezlie. "Call Narrative Project: An Examination of Struggle and Spiritual Formation in Female Seminarians of the African Diaspora." DMin diss., Alliance Theological Seminary, 2014.

Koh-Butler, Amelia. "Getting Back Up in the Saddle." Unpublished essay. Fuller Theological Seminary, 2014.

Lee-Barnwell, Michele. *Neither Complementarian nor Egalitarian: A Kingdom Corrective to the Evangelical Gender Debate*. Grand Rapids: Baker Academic, 2014.

Lim, Siew Pik. "Touch Not the Lord's Anointed: Toxic Leaders and Reflexive Followers in Pentecostal Charismatic Churches in Asia." PhD diss., Fuller Theological Seminary, 2014.

Lingenfelter, Sherwood G. "Defining Institutional Realities: The Myth of the Right Form." In *The Three Tasks of Leadership: Worldly Wisdom for Pastoral Leaders*, edited by Eric O. Jacobsen, 55–67. Grand Rapids: Eerdmans, 2009.

———. *Leading Cross-Culturally: Covenant Relationships for Effective Christian Leadership*. Grand Rapids: Baker Academic, 2008.

———, ed. *Re-Visioning Leadership: Essays on Learning from Leadership Failure*. 2018. http://infoguides.fuller.edu/lingenfelter/current_research.

Lingenfelter, Sherwood G., and Marvin K. Mayers. *Ministering Cross-Culturally: A Model for Effective Personal Relationships*. Grand Rapids: Baker Academic, 2016.

Ortberg, John. "A Leader's Greatest Fear." *A Taste of the Summit*. Video. http://www.willowcreek.com/events/leadership/tots.asp.

Osborne, Larry. *Sticky Teams*. Grand Rapids: Zondervan, 2010.

Parks, Sharon Daloz. *Leadership Can Be Taught: A Bold Approach for a Complex World*. Boston: Harvard Business School Press, 2005.

Plueddemann, James E. *Leading across Cultures: Effective Ministry and Mission in the Global Church*. Downers Grove: IVP Academic, 2009.

Shuster, Marguerite. *Power, Pathology, Paradox: The Dynamics of Evil and Good*. Grand Rapids: Zondervan, 1987.

Sunquist, Scott W. *Understanding Christian Mission: Participation in Suffering and Glory*. Grand Rapids: Baker Academic, 2013.

Trebesch, Shelley G. *Made to Flourish: Beyond Quick Fixes to a Thriving Organization*. Downers Grove: InterVarsity, 2015.

Webster, Noah. *Webster's New Universal Unabridged Dictionary*. New York: Simon & Schuster, 1979.

Willard, Dallas. *The Divine Conspiracy: Rediscovering Our Hidden Life in God*. HarperSanFrancisco, 1998.